EVERYTHING YOU ALWAYS SUSPECTED

TRUE ABOUT ADVERTISING

Martyn Forrester, an ex-copywriter for various
well-known advertising agencies, has written a
number of books on subjects as diverse as
elephants, poseurs, survival and street credi-
bility. *Everything You Always Suspected Was
True About Advertising* is his bravest venture
so far. He lives in south London with his wife,
two daughters and a libel lawyer.

Everything you always suspected was true about advertising

BUT WERE TOO LEGAL, DECENT AND HONEST TO ASK

MARTYN FORRESTER

FONTANA/Collins

First published by Roger Houghton in 1987
First issued in Fontana Paperbacks 1988

© Martyn Forrester 1987

Printed and bound in Great Britain by
William Collins Sons & Co. Ltd, Glasgow

Acknowledgement

I would like to thank the 147 adpeople who gave unstintingly of their time, wit and wisdom in order to help me write this book, in the only way they know how – over a lunch table.

Thanks to their forthright candour, I guarantee that everything you are about to learn about advertising can fight the symptoms of disbelief with regular reading.

A few inaccuracies may have crept in during the transcription of the manuscript from the original tablecloths, napkins and backs of Marlboro packets, but the final typescript was rigorously checked by a panel of housewives from Purley.

Any inaccuracies that remain are due purely to the settling of contents during transit, to selective memory, and to the fact that I've just had a jolly good lunch.

Martyn Forrester
Langan's
1987

An important message to you from the author

Dear Reader,

What a magnificent decade it has been so far for the advertising agencies of Britain; with billions of pounds being spent each year on posters, brochures, ads, TV commercials and sales letters like this one with lots of underlining, italics, different coloured inks, multi-width margins and Johnson Boxes with asterisks, many agencies report profits improved by as much as 100 per cent a year!

To celebrate our tremendous success, we now offer you the unique chance to study this sumptuously bound volume in the comfort of your own home.

*LEARN HOW TO ... earn a telephone number salary and a Porsche
... have the most fun you can with your clothes on
... eat, drink, love, travel – and put it all down to expenses

*LEARN WHY ... pythons always look so docile in TV commercials
... penguins enjoy talking into telephones
... a certain brand of toffee was so successful because it reminded female consumers of oral sex

PLUS! Everything else you always suspected was true about working in the greatest industry since sliced bread.

Read on quickly to avoid disappointment.

PS Don't forget, this privileged offer of life-enhancing insights is only being made to certain discerning members of the book-buying public.

PPS Make absolutely sure that you remember to use both a PS and a PPS – it's called 'Putting The Hot Pants On The Hooker' and it helps pull millions more punters.

'Advertising is riddled with ethics'
Robin Wight

'Advertising is the rattling of a stick inside a swill bucket'
George Orwell

Contents

Advertising: It's So Bracing

There are just 15,000 workers in the entire British advertising industry, and that includes the cleaners. Many other people depend on it for their livelihoods – restaurateurs and publicans, mostly. But it is essentially about this dedicated force of 15,000 hard-working professionals – and the billions of pounds of advertising expenditure that they handle each year – that this book is written.

You'll notice two things about it as you read on. The first is that it deals only with British advertising. This is because no other nation produces ads worth talking about – not even America, the former United States of Advertising. The second is that it deals only with advertising that has been paid for as recognisable advertising – and so we won't be talking about the sort of 'product placement' deals that had Steven Spielberg rubbing our noses in JVC, Toyota and Pepsi in *Back To The Future.*

An Advertising Association survey has revealed that 77 per cent of Britons approve of advertising 'a little or a lot'. It was a different story twenty years ago. Then, the same percentage were moaning that commercials actively spoiled their telly-viewing lives. People nowadays are increasingly involved in advertising. T-shirts are covered in it. Comedians make jokes about it. Television and radio series are based on it. Newspapers and magazines carry articles about the new Oxo family, or where the Guinness toucan has flown to – indeed, where the entire Guinness account has flown to. Football crowds know a nice jingle when they hear one, Cyril. Cinema-goers know a nice bottom when they see one, and male models who take their jeans off in launderettes become instant celebrities. But best of all, tell your fellow guests at a dinner party that you work in advertising, and they no longer look at you as if you were an unpleasant substance they'd just found on their shoes.

For all this, we must give credit to Mrs Thatcher. Thanks to her, most people in this country can now name at least one agency: Saatchi and Saatchi (even though it is, in fact, at least twenty-seven agencies). But of Saatchi's, less later.

OVERHEARD IN THE CITY

'You won't go far wrong if you follow the edicts of David Ogilvy. But you won't necessarily produce anything brilliant, either.'

OVERHEARD UPSTAIRS AT LANGAN'S

'I taught him everything he knows. Not everything *I* know, but everything *he* knows . . .'

OVERHEARD IN SOHO SQUARE

'We call Ted Bates the mushroom agency. They keep us in the dark, and feed us bullshit.'

Go To Work on an Ego

A year or two ago, the managing director of a major agency decided to give one of his account men The Big E. Summoned to the great man's office, the exec braced himself for the worst and walked in. The boss, who was conducting a telephone conversation at that moment, looked up at his quivering employee, said: 'You're fired', and carried on with his call. Then, after a moment's reflection, he looked up again and said: 'Want to know why? No good.' And that was that. And that, ladies and gentlemen, is what it's like to work in advertising.

As any psychiatrist will tell you, advertising scores higher on the stressometer than just about any other job you care to name. It's not like the rest of British industry, which has no concept of delivery dates or of wanting to keep a customer's business. In advertising, if you lose a client, you'll probably lose your job. So everybody delivers on time, and that usually means working late, taking work home, working weekends. Probably half the people in advertising put in regular 12-hour days. They burn midnight oil. And they compete: not only against other agencies, but against themselves. You are constantly selling yourself in an agency. Your skills are on trial, and so is your personality. Like a film director, you are only as good as your last piece of work. No wonder everyone's pissed all the time. No wonder everyone needs Porsche upholstery to cushion the ride.

As any marriage guidance counsellor will surely tell you, adpeople's marriages are often very rocky indeed. The failure rate is high. Livers fail a lot too. Many adpeople are either alcoholics, or very nearly alcoholics. Stress is so high, in fact, that it's not unknown for psychologists to be called in to help people cope. In some offices, you can even get acupuncture as part of the package.

So why would anybody in their right mind want to join such a weird business in the first place? Ah. The truth is, they wouldn't. Advertising is an asylum for the manic, the neurotic, the psychotic, the aberrant, a haven for poseurs. It provides a forum for debauchery and excess, an arena within which a mixed bag of creative and libidinous people can try to get inside each others' pants whilst drinking each other under the boardroom table.

Talking of bags, let's start our introduction to the *Dramatis Personae* of an agency by meeting the market researchers. They're the ladies with clipboards who show your ads to panels of housewives from Purley, who do their very best to sink the campaign without trace. That's all you need to know about them.

Clients are the people who finance the agency payroll, and as such are Very Important People. They demand brilliant advertising from you, and if a campaign does get past the Purley selection panel, they are the people who will then cost-cut it down from a 40-second TV commercial to a 20 cm × 2 column ad in the *Wandsworth Gazette*.

Clients need special people to look after them – called account handlers, account execs, suits or reps. Clients love them because they are so good at carrying bags, hailing taxis and picking up the restaurant bill. These demanding functions apart, their only other job is to sell the creative department's work to the client and to keep the client happy – two simple tasks which are frequently mutually exclusive.

One of the greatest account men of all time is Frank Lowe, who now heads up his own agency, Lowe Howard-Spink Marschalk. Lowe once went off to present some work to a client and on his return proudly held up the ad and announced: 'Good news. He bought it.' The creative man noticed at this point that Lowe was actually holding the ad upside down.

'Frank,' he said, 'it's supposed to be the other way up.'

'Is it?' said Lowe. 'Never mind. That's how I sold it, anyway.'

Art buyers have a much tougher time of it. They liaise between the agency and outside suppliers, usually in dimly lit corners of expensive restaurants and underground car parks. They drive Mercs, and live with hot and cold running noughts in the more fashionable areas of Holland Park and Notting Hill.

Planners are the new intelligentsia of advertising, taking over the mantle traditionally held by the chairman's wife. They're all into concept boards and documents, and things like 'gap analysis'; if 90 per cent of tea drinkers like hot tea and 40 per cent like iced tea, then a planner is the person who will suggest that there must be a yawning gap in the marketplace for lukewarm tea.

Planners are only marginally better company than the people who inhabit the media floor – mediamen, who drink gallons of real ale, play lots of arrows, and can start talking readership statistics faster than you can say: 'Gosh, is that the time? I really must be going . . .' Women mediamen are a totally different proposition, usually being members of a team because they have looks that will wow the client. But beware, they often also have brains that would wow an IBM mainframe.

Progress chasers – or production handlers – are in charge of getting the right things to the right people at the right time. A typical day for them will therefore start with a bollocking by an art buyer, end with a bollocking by a creative team, and in between be filled with bollockings by media people, planners, account handlers and the girls in the canteen. Apart from being everybody's scapegoats, their only other jobs are to score goals for the agency football team, and to sing 'Ere we go, 'ere we go, 'ere we go' at the Christmas party – usually during the chairman's speech.

Creatives are almost the top people in the agency. They're bought and sold like footballers, with transfer fees to match. According to a survey in 1985 by *Campaign*, the industry journal, less than two-thirds of creatives stay in the same agency for a full year. A third of agencies lose half their creative staff within twelve months.

In the creative department there are copywriters and there are art directors. Copywriters are the ones with the ideas, and art directors are the ones who draw them up. Copywriters are the ones who go on to write *Catch 22* or *Real Men Don't Eat Quiche*, or who invent Pet Rocks and become millionaires. In his days at Ford, Lee Iacocca considered his copywriter from JWT so essential that he'd have him sitting in at his more important meetings. That's why copywriters get the biggest salaries. But there is, as ever, a drawback. Art directors get laid more.

Which nearly brings us to the most important person in the agency. But first, a story about creatives. Creatives aren't allowed near clients very much, because they tend to grab their noses, hurl abuse, even bite them. Clients love this, of course. An account man was once on his way to a meeting when he spotted one of the senior creatives on the account, a writer with long wild hair, who was busy rolling a cigarette. 'Come and do that in the meeting,' the account man said, 'they love that sort of thing.'

This story concerns a brilliant copywriter who, at the time, had a rather tough-looking Yorkshireman as his art director. The team were given the job of doing a campaign for a Glenn Miller compilation album on behalf of a record-producing client. The trouble with the album was that it seemed to be twice as expensive as, and contain half the number of tracks of, any other Glenn Miller compilation album – of which there were dozens. It was doomed to failure from the start, and the art director said so. Never one to turn down a challenge, however, they attacked the task with gusto. They thought of a name for the album, designed a cover for it, and wrote a script. Shot very moodily and beautifully, the commercial showed a Second World War plane taking off into thick, foreboding fog. . . .

When the moment came to present the finished film, one of the clients decided he knew a thing or two about aeroplanes. 'That plane in the commercial had very small fuel tanks,' he said, 'and it couldn't have made it to France.'

With a sharp intake of breath, the art director replied: 'Well it f***ing didn't, did it, sunbeam?'

History relates that the team were moved off the business pretty sharpish, and as to the success of the commercial: if you know anyone who wants a job-lot of Glenn Miller compilation albums, there's a warehouseful somewhere in London.

And now, a few words about the single (or married, it makes no difference) most important person in the whole agency.

Your secretary.

She of the short skirt and the big smile, the baggy leather jacket and the bright designer Walkman with 'Girls Just Wanna Have Fun' on continuous loop. She who can talk till the cows come home about clothes, make-up, jewellery, highlights, designer drugs, and in which position the creative director likes it best. She who goes well with the debonair human chandeliers of the account handling floor, and who goes equally well on the artistic twisted Wilton of the creative floor. She who models herself heavily on the Duchess of York, Madonna, Kelly Emberg. She who lives in Annabel's, Morton's, the Hippodrome. She who does aerobics, who skis, who says 'absolutely' a lot. She, above all, who knows secrets – enough to make her indispensable on trips to LA in exchange for her silence. And if every secretary in the agency was laid end to end, well, it wouldn't be for the first time.

So there you have it. The group of people whose entire lives are dedicated to making other people's products and services look charming, human, warm, attractive, desirable . . . or your money back.

Like the man said, nice work if you can get it.

OVERHEARD IN THE JUNGLE
'Advertising is a people business. So is cannibalism.'

OVERHEARD IN MD'S OFFICE
'It's only an ad.'

OVERHEARD IN BERKELEY SQUARE
'Paranoia has gone right to the top. God thinks he's Charles Saatchi.'

Men/Women Wanted For Hazardous Journey. Constant Danger, Safe Return Doubtful. Honour and Recognition in Case of Success

By this time tomorrow, you too could have a job in advertising. And by the same time the day after, you could have lost it again. For this you would give up the security of being, say, a polar explorer?

If you want to be an account exec, the application procedure is very straightforward. Go to either Oxford or Cambridge, or have a dad who owns the agency (or who is a major client – it amounts to the same thing).

On the creative side, entry is rather more difficult. Every year, at least 500 hopefuls are chasing twenty jobs or fewer. The odds are, well, who knows, creative people aren't good at arithmetic. Stacked against you, anyway. You can still bludgeon your way in, though, by laying siege to creative directors with collections of speculative ads – called your 'portfolio' or 'book'. Or you can pull a stunt that gets you into *Campaign*. Or you can send out a mailer. Or produce a brochure. Or go to a headhunter. Or you can even, as one writer did a few years ago, go to a creative director, claim to have leukaemia, and beg for the chance to spend the last few months of your life working as a copywriter. The creative director will oblige, but will then get suspicious when you're still around after a year. So you will then go on a pilgrimage to Lourdes and come back claiming a miracle. The creative director will then go on a pilgrimage to his filing cabinet and present you with a P45.

One of the most popular ways into a creative department is still by simply ripping off someone else's work and presenting it as your own. Use this method sparingly, however, and do try to check that the ads you're showing this creative director weren't done by him in the first place.

Creative directors are experts at spotting such techniques, mostly because they've pulled the same stunts themselves. One famous creative director arrived from across the water many years ago with a book composed almost entirely of ads he'd ripped out of the Sunday supplements. He got a job at once.

You could always send off a CV and letter to agencies in the hope that they'll let you do a copy test. In today's climate, though, it's unlikely that a mere letter will be enough to get you an interview. A creative mailer is a much better idea. It might even win you an award or two. One writer mailed out an asbestos glove a few years ago that was overprinted with the message: 'To be worn when handling my portfolio.' It won him a D&AD (Designers & Art Directors Association) gold and silver, and got him a job at JWT. The cover of another creative's mailer read 'For the next few weeks I'll be at JWT Manchester ...' Inside was a little Subbuteo footballer, and the words: '... working on a little pitch.' It got him a D&AD mention and a job at TBWA.

Others have succeeded by putting up posters behind each lavatory door in the agency, that said: 'Hire the team that catches the rest of the agency with its pants down.' Or by sending an inflated balloon with a pin attached. When the balloon was burst, out dropped a note that said: 'If this is the biggest bang you've had all year out of advertising, you ought to see my portfolio.' Another mailer showed a sad-looking goldfish, with the message: 'Phone this number and ask for Bob the Frog. No cops and no funny stuff. Fail to cooperate by 1st July and the goldfish eats lead.' Give that man a cigar.

One managing director once received a letter from an aspiring account exec which began 'Dear Uncle David', and went on to say, 'Father suggested I tell you how much I would like to get involved in the account handling side of advertising ...' The writer of the letter was totally unknown to the agency recipient, but he got his interview.

The moment they do get into an agency, most people seem to start writing books, plays, songs and material for 'Spitting Image'. Of the 15,000 people who work in advertising, maybe 1,500 are creatives. Of these, just about every other one seems to be a published author.

If they don't write books, they go on to direct commercials and feature films. Ridley Scott (*Blade Runner*), Hugh Hudson (*Chariots of Fire*), Alan Parker (*Midnight Express*) and Adrian Lyne (*Flashdance*) all cut their teeth in the advertising business.

As you might expect for people who deal all the time with television, admen have also found their way onto the small screen. David Edwards invented SuperTed. Roger Hargreaves invented the Mr Men whilst creative director at FCB in 1971. Terry Howard wrote 'The Other 'Arf', and is still creative director at Ayer Barker. Richard Stilgoe was a copywriter at JWT before Andrew Lloyd Webber was even born and was one of the first creatives ever to appear in one of his own commercials – one for Dubonnet, directed by Hugh Hudson in 1975.

And then we come to the real heavyweight old boys of advertising . . .

Salman Rushdie's Booker Prize-winning *Midnight's Children* was written while he was a copywriter at Ayer Barker. Apart from *Midnight's Children*, Rushdie will probably be best remembered as the author of the line 'That'll Do Nicely' for American Express.

Dorothy L. Sayers worked at Benson's, and invented the Guinness toucan. She also wrote the immortal lines:

> If he can say as you can
> Guinness is good for you,
> How grand to be a Toucan
> Just think what two can do.

William Trevor wrote *The Old Boys* when at Notley's. Jack Rosenthal (*The Barmitzvah Boy, P'Tang, Yang, Kipperbang*) used to work at Osborne Peacock in Manchester. Fay Weldon devised the line 'Happiness Is Egg-shaped' while working at Mather & Crowther. James Herbert and Len Deighton used to work in advertising. So did the poets Edward Lucie-Smith,

Gavin Ewart, Peter Porter and Peter Redgrove. The poet Edwin Brock is still at Ogilvy and Mather, where he invented the phrase 'Pub Grub'.

Not everyone who jumps or is pushed takes up the pen. Tim Drake and Tim Pluck had a difference of opinion with their agency and went off and started the highly successful Cobra chain of Sportswear shops. Bob Payton left JWT and started a little place called the Chicago Pizza Pie Factory, that did so well that he also opened the Rib Shack, that did so well that he also opened Payton's Plaice. Most adpeople, though, seem to leave and buy farms – presumably because they have become so accustomed to the smell of bullshit.

OVERHEARD IN THE MD'S OFFICE

'Don't worry. We're just redecorating your office.'

OVERHEARD IN CLIENT'S CAB

'That new creative director is either crazy or both.'

OVERHEARD IN BOARDROOM

MALE BOARD DIRECTOR TO NEWLY APPOINTED WOMAN DIRECTOR: 'I don't like employing women. When you push them they always burst into tears.'

WOMAN DIRECTOR: 'Oh really? That's just the problem I have with my junior account men.'

The Night of the Long Envelopes

Firing usually takes about ten minutes on a Friday afternoon. Sometimes, however, the process is handled rather more subtly; like, the offices are redecorated and reallocated, and you find that your name simply doesn't appear on the new floor plan. Or you come back from a shoot to discover that your desk has disappeared. Or that it's there, but there's somebody else sitting at it.

By and large, though, it's the Friday afternoon number. That gives you plenty of time to contact your lawyer over the weekend, and for him to confirm that the golden parachute they're slipping you is so damned big it would be madness to go anywhere near an Industrial Tribunal. Thus you arrive at the office all sweetness and cooperation on Monday morning, ready to discuss an extra 'good behaviour' payment for telling clients and *Campaign* that it was an amicable split, and whether it's all right if you hang on to the company motor for six months or so. (One agency was so embarrassed about firing someone that they agreed to sell a car to him for £1!)

The biggest blood-baths occur when a new creative director arrives. The new-generals-need-new-lieutenants syndrome takes over with a vengeance. Shivers run through the department – and we're talking the kind of shivers that register on the Richter scale. To brown-nose or not to brown-nose, that is usually the question, or whether 'tis nobler to simply keep thy head down. Whichever, stand by for the slings and arrows, mostly in thy back.

'You Too Can Have Bodycopy
Like Mine'

12.35pm

On your desk in front of you is The Brief.

A creative brief consists of simple, clear, concise answers to four very important questions:

What is the problem or opportunity?
What do we expect the advertising to do?
Whose behaviour are we trying to affect?
And what is the single most important thing we want people to take from the advertising?

The account execs and planners will then pad out, lard and generally swamp this information with all sorts of marketing jargon, hearsay, guesses, conjectures, recommendations, queries and inch-thick support documents. It'll take you at least one lunch to strip away all the deadwood – that's why they put it there. Having got to the point where the brief is acceptable, however, there's not much more room for manoeuvre. Very little alternative, in fact, to sitting down somewhere (preferably Paris) and actually cracking it.

When knocking out your ad or TV script don't hesitate to pay homage to feature films. *Blade Runner* is always good value, and so was Carl Reiner's *Dead Men Don't Wear Plaid*: that's where one agency got their award-winning idea from for the

Holsten Pils commercials with Griff Rhys-Jones. And as for the Levi 501s commercial with teen throb Nick Kamen stripping off in a launderette, well, Toyah Wilcox did it first, back in 1981, in Derek Jarman's film *Jubilee*.

If such inspirations fail to solve your problems, you can always go for the old thinking-alike-of-great-minds trick. The commercial which showed a 7 Series BMW being driven through a graveyard of other cars is a good example of this phenomenon. It bears more than a passing resemblance to an Australian commercial for Volvo, produced five years previously. Even the music sounds familiar . . .

Some other quite remarkable coincidences can happen in advertising. Like the ad for New Balance sports shoes, featuring an X-rayed foot, which was remarkably similar to the award-winning ad for Nike sports shoes, already published in the USA, which featured an X-rayed foot. Then there was the remarkable similarity between the ad for the Royal United Kingdom Beneficent Association, featuring a wallet and a £10 note with Florence Nightingale on it, and the ad for the Red Cross that appeared a bit later, featuring a wallet and a £10 note with Florence Nightingale on it. Or the ad for the Royal Viking Line, featuring a backdrop of the Grand Canal in Venice with a cruise liner on the horizon, which was remarkably similar to the ad for P & O which appeared a month later, and which featured a backdrop of the Grand Canal in Venice with a cruise liner on the horizon. But surely one of the greatest coincidences of all time is the similarity between the ages-old American 'To Peggy' ad for Hamilton watches, and the award-winning British 'Dear Dad' ad for Chivas Regal.

If all else fails there are always various ways out of the predicament – depending on which country you're in. In America, get the cast to sing. In France or Scandinavia (except Sweden: the Swedes don't allow TV commercials), just get them to take their clothes off. In Britain, simply bolt on a joke or two. Failing a joke, is there anything else you can bolt on? What about a nice fifties rock 'n' roll classic, for example, or a memorable little trick like making everybody turn upside down at the end and explode?

If at first you don't succeed, go back to your annuals and *Headlines Monthly*. Try looking at the product the right way. These days, dog food isn't dog food, for heaven's sake – it's what fuels that quintessential symbol of the happy nuclear family, the happy family dog. Holidays aren't holidays – they're opportunities for aforesaid nuclear family to seek individual and group fulfilment on a sunlit beach. Write your ad accordingly.

And if even this fails, use one of the formulae. Take the product benefit, exaggerate it, dramatise it, blow it up out of all proportion. If your apple drink has a strong smell, have Frenchmen falling off their bikes on the other side of the Channel because of it. If your crisps are crunchy, have whole buildings collapsing because of the noise. You know the sort of thing. Or simply take a historical or literary situation or problem (Robert the Bruce and the spider, King Alfred and the cakes, The Three Bears, Henry the Eighth), add your product and a few puns, and show how it would have resolved the problem. It's a winner every time.

Either way, you'll end up with a highly entertaining film that talks to other creatives and wins barrow-loads of awards . . . and a product whose name no punter can remember.

12.45pm

So now it's time to go to lunch. When you get back, we'll briefly mug up the techniques and approaches that you'll need if your ads, too, are to be legal, decent, honest and truthful . . .

OVERHEARD AT CLIENT MEETING

'This campaign fills a much needed gap.'

MEMO FROM MD TO CREATIVE DEPARTMENT

Would everyone please stop spending all morning gazing out of the window. Leave yourselves something to do in the afternoon.'

'My Brain Says it's Time to go Back to the Office, but my Body Says Stay and Have Another Drink . . .'

In advertising the factory hooter goes at 12.45, and the rest of the day is then given over to redistributing the agency's wealth amonst the nation's needy waiters, waitresses, chefs – and Peter Langan.

From the business point of view there is no doubt that it is an immensely functional time of day. It comes after a gap of over four hours since one's last meeting, over breakfast at the Connaught.

It is the time for account directors to cement alliances and swing deals and a time for account execs to sell your creative work to clients. It is the time when account men take you out to say thank you for a job well done, and it is the time when you take the account men to say sorry for a job not quite done yet, but it will be by tomorrow, honest guv. It is the time when suppliers say thank you for giving them the opportunity to demonstrate their skills (at slipping brown envelopes under the table), and it is the time when film directors say thank you for giving them the opportunity to write your script for you. It is the time for creative directors to hire new faces during a three-hour session at the Caprice, and it is the time for them to fire old ones during a four-hour thrash at the Ritz. It is the time, above all else, for well-meaning creatives to whisk difficult female clients or haughty agency PAs off to Langan's, to get them to lower their reserve, or, better still, their Calvin Klein underwear.

It is, of course, lunchtime – and woebetide the poor wretch whose diary is not crammed full with them. The penalty is hours of walking the streets or hiding in cinemas, anxiously checking

one's watch until 3.15 comes round and it is respectable – just –
to slink back into the agency with a bottle of chilled Chablis to
sip quietly with one's secretary until it's opening time, party
time, Zanzibar time or plain old dinner time. Either that, or a
morning spent composing a damned good excuse to explain
the sandwich and yoghurt at your desk, like: 'Recovering from
yesterday's thrash,' 'On my way to play Frank over at the RAC,'
or (better) 'Just waiting to talk to LA.'

You'll find a copy of Roget's *Thesaurus* on the office shelves
of every dedicated adman, together with certain other volumes
which are just as important to his professional success: *Michelin
France*; *Gault-Millau France*; *The Harpers & Queen London
Restaurant Guide*; *Gault-Millau London*; *The Good Food Guide*;
Egon Ronay, and *Gault-Millau New York*. 'Let's have lunch' is
perhaps the most used phrase in any advertising agency,
anywhere in the world.

Close on the heels of these immortal words come 'Let's have
a quick drink' (eight pints in the White Swan); 'Let's have a
quick pint and a sandwich' (eight pints in the White Swan and
no sandwich) or 'Let's just grab a quick snack' (two bottles of
sake in a sushi bar).

Whatever the form of the invitation, you can be sure of one
thing. And that is that you won't find a pair of admen sitting at a
window seat in Oxford Street, tucking into Wendyburgers and
large fries, or tackling two eggs on two toasts, with bacon,
sausage, tomato and cups of tea at the local greasy spoon. Like
other people need oxygen, advertising people need ceiling
fans, hand-calligraphed menus, and the strong possibility that
Dudley Moore will be on the adjacent table.

That's why every adperson worth his or her naturally dried
sea-salt will know that Frank Lowe and Princess Anne both
favour San Lorenzo's, that Peter Mead and Barbra Streisand can
be seen at Langan's, and that Dave Trott and the Duchess of
Argyll are habitués of Joe Allen's. For the same reason, account
execs eager to impress their clients will take them to Bagatelle
to see Bryan Ferry, to Odins to see David Hockney, or to the
Busabong or Mr Chow to clock Mick Jagger. Execs might also
care to note that the following sightings have been regularly
reported by royalty-conscious colleagues: The Duke and
Duchess of York at Cecconi's, The Queen Mother at Bewick's,
Prince Charles at Annabel's and Don White at the Ritz.

Helping your client to be seen in the best restaurants is not enough: he'll want to be seen at the best tables, too – nearly always as close to Lichfield, Geldof or the main door as possible; or a window, if it's Le Tour d'Argent in Paris. Every restaurant has its leper colony. And as a committed adluncher you will know them all: the main dining room at the Four Seasons in New York (power lunches are consumed in the panelled grill room); upstairs at Langan's. You would rather vomit down your client's wife's cleavage than allow yourself to be seated in such Siberias.

As an employee who's been invited out to lunch, the restaurant's standing in the league table of perceived trendiness can provide you with a pretty good idea of what's going to be on the agenda. The trendier and more fashionable the restaurant, the more content your host obviously is to be seen with you. So if it's Moscow's, L'Escargot, the Neal Street Restaurant or Langan's (downstairs), stand by for a decent pay rise and a new car. But if it's the Savoy, the Ritz, the Meridiana, or Langan's (upstairs), make sure you change into a pair of baggy brown cords before you leave the agency. . . .

3.30pm. And now, if you're lying comfortably, we present:

OVERHEARD AT THE CAPRICE

AGENCY MAN: 'I'll have the grilled breast of lamb.'
WAITER: 'And how would sir like it cooked?'
AGENCY MAN: 'Properly.'

OVERHEARD IN DIRECTOR'S LIMO

'Of course I've known what it is to be hungry, but I've always gone straight to Langan's.'

How to Press Buttons and Influence People

Every consumer has weaknesses. Every consumer has deep-seated emotional needs and desires and vulnerabilities. The job of an advertising agency is to isolate and identify these emotional cuts and grazes, and then to rub on lots of ads that say 'there, there' – that soothe, or gratify, or relieve.

'Advertising deals in open sores,' Jerry Della Femina once said. 'Fear. Greed. Anger. Hostility. You name the dwarfs and we play on every one. We play on all the emotions and on all the problems, from not getting ahead ... to the desire to be one of the crowd. Everyone has a button. If enough people have the same button, you have a successful ad and a successful product.'

So you get McDonald's or Coca Cola running warm, bungy, cuddly commercials that stress togetherness and community and fill gaps in people's lives. You get brands of whisky or chocolates that position themselves as very up-market and touch the exposed nerves of insecure social climbers. And you get Marlboro or Camel ads that stress rugged, macho individuality and press all the right buttons with young smokers in search of an identity.

All you have to do is look at the produce or service you're selling and work out which of the consumer's weak, vulnerable and insecure buttons you should be pressing. To help you, there now follows a complete checklist of everything the psychologists tell us we need to know about human character and personality:

Punters like money, status, comfort, sex, toys, games,

possessions. They hate any suggestion that they are being deprived of any of these things.

Punters like knowledge, new information, practical and DIY skills. They like to be able to help themselves. They hate any suggestion that they are being deprived of any of these things.

Punters like security, protection, having reserves. They hate any suggestion that they are being deprived of any of these things; they also hate discomfort, embarrassment, risk, worry, hassle.

Punters like to feel fulfilled, creative, individual, happy, self-confident. They hate any suggestion that they are being deprived of any of these things; they like to get away, to escape, to avoid pressures and big decisions.

Punters like to be accepted, to be popular, to receive praise, to be thought of as stylish, fashionable, up-to-date. Some like to be seen as authoritative or respectable, others as notorious or unrespectable. Some even like to be seen to be helping others.

Punters like to keep up with the Joneses, or even better, to be one-up on them. They like to be efficient, smart, sensible, organised, improved, faster, to be forewarned, to know something before others do. They like to feel cosy, satisfied, smug.

They like to be liked.

And as any editor of the *Sun* will tell you, they also like:

animals	royalty
babies	sex
cars	sport
disasters	war
entertainment	weddings

Do an ad around any of these subjects (except royalty – you're not allowed to use the royals in ads) and you're talking gold.

So much for consumer psychographics. Now let's get down to the nitty-gritty: the techniques and approaches that are going to earn you a ticket to Cannes and the award ceremonies.

In pride of place, we have The Weasel – the word that effectively negates everything else that follows. Hot favourite is 'helps', as in 'helps control tooth decay'. 'Probably' is also rather good, as in 'probably the best lager in the world'. So, too, are 'virtually', 'enriched', 'fortified', 'refreshes', 'can be', 'up to', 'often'. You name it, a copywriter can make a positive statement, then find a weasel to disclaim it.

Let's consider an example. 'Helps fight the symptoms of tooth decay with regular use.' Does that mean 'stops tooth decay'? Oh come on now. Count the weasels:
'Helps' – goes an almost immeasurably small way towards,
'fight' – opposing, but certainly not overcoming,
'the symptoms' – the symptoms, and that's all, of tooth decay,
'with regular use' – as long as you buy lots of it.
That's four weasels in all – a real tribute to the copywriter concerned.

Now let's take a 'me-too' product like mineral water (or 'designer water', as it should really be called) and apply the techniques to it as we go through them. Our product is *Sparkling Old Thames Water*, and a good weasly claim would be: 'Can often help alleviate the symptoms of digestive disorder.'

2. *'Sparkling Old Thames Water quenches thirst faster.'*
The Unfinished Symphony – the ad that claims the product is better or contains more of something, but leaves the comparison uncompleted. As in: 'Persil Washes Whiter' . . . than what?
'We'll Take More Care Of You' . . . than whom?

3. *'Only Sparkling Old Thames Water has that unique Thames heritage.'*
The Spurious Uniqueness Claim – an excellent long-stop, that never fails. All you have to do is find the unique property of your product, or even invent one. Add a molecule of something or other to your soap powder, and you can say: 'There's nothing like new blue Sudz', or 'Only Sudz has the Perma-Crease formula'.

4. *'Sparkling Old Thames Water. The Thirst Quencher.'*
The Water Is Wet Announcement – the claim that your lager refreshes, your soap powder washes, or some other statement of the blindingly obvious that also applies to every other brand in the category.

5. *"'Fish don't procreate in Sparkling Old Thames Water," says discerning drinker W. C. Fields.'*
The Testimonial. Quite good, but do you really imagine that Lulu shops out of the Freemans catalogue, that Alan Whicker uses a Barclaycard rather than gold Amex, that James Hunt drives a Honda, that Judith Chalmers has Draylon curtains, or that John McEnroe uses Bic razors? You cannot be serious.

6. *'Sparkling Old Thames Water. The water with the two tributary taste.'*
The So What? claim. You hear it or you read it, and you say, So what? 'Twice the vitamins of other breakfast cereals.' So what? Is that twice as good for your body?

7. *'The one that makes sensible drinking delicious. Take just one sip and you're gliding through the timeless landscape of Olde Englande.'*
The Eh What? Lots of lovely words, all of them colourful but totally meaningless. Often crammed with up to 100 per cent natural weasels.

8. *'Shouldn't your family be drinking the natural goodness of Sparkling Old Thames Water?'*
The Rhetorical Question – to which you're supposed to answer yes. As in: 'Wouldn't You Rather Be Hemeling?' or 'Are You Going Home To A Guinness?'

9. *'Re-cycled six times for BMA purity.'*
The Blind-'Em-With-Science. Jolly good wheeze this one – just wheel out a bit of scientific proof, a few numbers or percentages, or a boffin-boggling mystery ingredient like ZP11 or WD40.

10. *'The water your discerning palate insists on – the water your distinguished table demands.'*
The Flattery-Gets-You-Everywhere. Poor weak creatures that we are, we fall for a compliment every time.

11. *'Britain's top wine taster tells how to choose water.'*
Or: Very famous traveller tells why to choose Barclaycard
Or: Very famous policeman tells why to choose Goodyear tyres

Or: Very famous punk tells why to choose Nat-West Bank

12. *'OWN YOUR OWN RIVER! Win this fabulous Sparkling Old Thames Water contest and your prize is your very own tributary of the Piddle!'*
Contests can be good, but beware of money being hived off into the prize fund. The budget belongs in the pocket of the agency, not that of some professional competition entrant from Milton Keynes.

13. *'Your guide to the week's best water.'*
(Under pic of seven Sparkling Old Thames Water, each subtitled 'Monday', 'Tuesday', etc.)
Many clients insist that you advertise their entire product range in one go. They're the same sort of client who will say, 'I paid for this bloody space, and I want it filled with ink – got it?' Fire them. If our water client insists for some reason on showing lots of bottles, then the solution above is rather elegant, if not exactly a gem.

14. *'The one with the dinner party taste.'*
This wholesome device is called 'Word Collision'. You can put together two or three words that you don't expect to see together, and hey presto! – you've got yourself a headline. You could have 'Dressier Dressing-Gowns'. 'Sockier Socks'. 'Armchair Whisky'. 'Jealous Ketchup'.

15. *'Sparkling Old Thames Water. The Table Water.'*
Simply give the product another name. Volkswagen did it with the 'Bug', and it didn't do them any harm.

16. *'You won't find a more palatable water anywhere.'*
Or: Never Knowingly Undersold.
Or: Find a cheaper one anywhere and we'll refund the difference. The challenge technique can be excellent, but check first that you're not standing on quicksand, productwise.

17. *'I have seen the Mississippi. That is muddy water. I have seen the St Lawrence. That is crystal water. But the Thames is liquid history.' John Burns 1858-1943*
The quotation technique, first port of call of the

second-rate writer. All a real copywriter needs on his desk is a green Pentel, a yellow pad, and the phone number of a young team who'll do anything for a cheap lunch. If you are a client and you spot a book of quotations in the creative department, turn at once to the chapter on 'Choosing A New Agency'.

18. *'Are you a secret aqua-holic?'*
The Quiz. Excellent, but can be generic. 'Answer ten simple questions and work out the date of your death' sells life insurance in general, not necessarily Albany Life.

19. *'A bottle a day keeps the liver specialist away.'*
If you're absolutely stumped for an idea, bung in the word 'day' – as seen in A Mars a day . . . Drinka Pinta Milka Day . . . Have you Macleaned your teeth today? . . . All over London from Friday.

20. *'Every bottle's been passed by the management.'*
The Guarantee. But make sure the promise is either totally believable, or totally preposterous – like the brilliant 'Every bubble's passed its fizzical'.

21. *'Come to Old Thames country.'*
Oh dear. The old Invent-A-Country trick. Marlboro Country. Birds Eye Country. Ribena Land. You should get a free adworld atlas with every pack.

22. *'Old Father Thames – your kids will love him.'*
If you can't invent a country, you can always have a bash at a character. Katie. Cap'n Birds Eye. The Kellogg's Tiger.

23. *'I was the laughing stock of our social circle – guests threw ordinary mineral water in my face.'*
The classic before-and-after technique, however cleverly disguised:
Pale girl: 'I wouldn't dream of spending money on sun-tan lotion.'
Brown girl: 'I can see that.'

24. *'Come on in, the water's lovely.'*
(Under pic of smiling chairman.)
When all else fails, use the client. What do clients think of the technique? 'Bootiful.'

25. *'What to look for in water.'*
(Pic of rival bottles plus our product: other brands
have flecks of horse manure floating in them.)
Straightforward product comparison. You should
be so lucky, getting a product that comes out
ahead in any sort of test.

26. *'We dumped this bottle of Sparkling Old Thames
Water into a steaming heap of pigs' manure for six
months, then drank it. That's how much you can
trust the bottle with the unique Clino-Seal screw
top.'*
Ladies and gentlemen, The Torture Test: Band-
Aids clinging to eggs in boiling water, Volvos
frozen in blocks of ice, K-nirps umbrellas that a
car-wash cannot k-nacker. It's the greatest technique on earth. If you're selling Band-Aids, Volvos
or K-nirps.

Other techniques include strip cartoons and topical ads, but it's
time now to move on to buzz words – another important part of
the copywriter's armoury. Use any (or all) of the following in
your headline and bodycopy and you'll be well on the way to an
advertising effectiveness award:

Now · Free · Secret · Magic · Mother · Unique · Announcing
Introducing · Save pounds · Money Off · Guarantee · Economy
Bargain · Sent direct from the manufacturer · Breakthrough
Offer closes today · New · Improved · More · Buy

Well, you're almost there. All you need now is a crash course in
ignoring punctuation and forgetting every bit of grammar you
ever learned, and you'll soon be doing tremendous. Here's two
examples. (Three, if you count 'Here's two'.)

* 'A computer so well thought out, it will help you perform any
task quicker.' (Digital Computers)

* 'Take away the movement, take away sound and what are you
left with? That's right a press ad.' (ITV's TV versus Press
campaign)

And if you can't see what's wrong with either of these, welcome
to the wonderful world of advertising. You are now ready to
write your very first ad . . . .

FORTY GRAND AND A PORSCHE.
HOW?

Plentiful things, verbs.

Except in ads.

And as any modern copywriter worth his expenses will tell you, that's virtually the only thing you need to know about writing ads.

Apart from making each sentence into a new paragraph, regardless of sense or rhythm.

And using clauses as complete sentences.

Which they aren't.

And starting lots of sentences with 'And'.

Or 'So'.

Or 'So that's why'.

Or 'Because'.

Or 'Or'.

Lots of car ads are written like this.

So were the award-winning ads for Healthcrafts.

Except for one paragraph.

'Animal fats and sugar were also rationed. Cutting the average consumption by almost a third.'

They put two sentences in one paragraph in that one.

And they shouldn't even be two separate sentences at all.

OVERHEARD IN AGENCY LIFT

'Their advertising is better than it looks.'

OVERHEARD AT STRINGFELLOW'S

MALE CLIENT: 'Just think of me as a north country, uncultured hick.'

FEMALE ACCOUNT EXEC: 'No problem.'

Parliamo Adspeak

There's only one language that admen understand besides money, and that's adspeak. What in a law firm, say, would be: 'Put forward the proposal and we'll gauge people's reactions,' becomes: 'Run it up the flagpole and we'll see who salutes.' What a journalist might call 'asking a few people their views' becomes 'dipstick research'. What an accountant might call an approximate figure, becomes a 'ball-park figure'. And an idea that a politician might describe as 'prominent' becomes something that 'sticks out like the balls on a bulldog'.

Everyday speech in an ad agency – in particular amongst the suits – is peppered with graphic language that has been borrowed from other fields – especially sport. Especially American sport, so that the speaker can let everyone know how terribly mid-Atlantic he or she is. And especially rough and tumble sport, to prove that advertising isn't as effete an industry as many people imagine. As a rule of thumb, if Hemingway did it, you can base your language on it. Big game fishing is a crowd puller. So is boxing. Or you could always try bull-fighting. Baseball used to be excellent: it gave us such gems as the now cringingly passé 'touch base' (as in 'Let's touch base later' instead of 'Let's meet later').

A board member of JWT is generally considered to be one of the finest exponents of the adspeak metaphor in the business, though sometimes they don't quite come out as planned: 'We'll leave him in a hammock of animated suspension' is an excellent and not uncommon example.

Classics (by others) include the splendid: 'Why not think of these ideas as building blocks to play tunes on?' The evocative: 'To be honest, I believe in putting all our eggs on the table.' And the quite magnificent: 'I think we've barely scratched the iceberg.' And there's more. There's the visual surrealism of: 'You can't just ease back on the throttle after a month or two – you need a full year to get your head above the trench.' The sinister undertones of: 'To me, it's all a bit of a knee-jerk reflex for plug-in impact.' And the mind-blowing majesty of: 'Once we've got our ducks in a row, it'll be gang-busters.'

If you can't find an opportunity to invent and use a graphic metaphor, Rule Two of adspeak states that you should try to make a verb out of something else. You will then be able to 'lavatorise' a conversation, to 'fascistise' a situation (yes, really), or (good American football one, this) to 'refridgerator the opposition'. Enough to make you opticalise red, isn't it?

But there's more. As they say in the rulebook, if you can't dazzle them with brilliance, baffle them with bullshit. (And if that doesn't work, try mumbling.) Researchers are particularly good at gobbledygook. Deep down they know they're a waste of space, and they strive to make amends by using important-sounding language.

The poor client has to sit at day-long tracking study meetings and listen to his chocolate bar being discussed in terms of 'shopping precinct intercept situations with a one-to-one interface with respondents' (people were interviewed one at a time outside Woolie's), or 'negatives thrown up in the sampling which were in the potential weight-gain-anxiety cluster, presenting a barrier to effective brand penetration' (some people said they wouldn't buy the choc bar because they were worried about getting fat). No wonder they're always so glad when it's lunchtime. No wonder, too, that some of it eventually rubs off on them: a marketing document for toilet tissue refers, if you please, to the 'lower sheet usage per task' of their fine product. Not even a researcher could top that, and you know what practitioners of genital manipulation with a view to self-gratification they are . . .

Say It With Slogans

Tell someone you work in advertising and the odds are 10 to 1 they'll say: 'Oo, is it hard thinking up all those slogans?'

But advertising isn't so much about slogans any more. Gone are the days of 'We're number two – We try harder' or 'You don't have to be Jewish to love Levy's Real Jewish Rye' or 'Beanz Meanz Heinz' or 'Sch ... you know who' – days when advertising was all about the consistent building of a brand personality in order to win over the public and shift product off the shelves. In the cold, de-personalised eighties, it's all about one-off ads that are designed to win golds or silvers. Before they disappear for ever, therefore, preserved here for posterity are twelve of the more cogent and thought-provoking slogans of all time.

★ When Should A Blonde Give In? (Clairol)
★ Perhaps We Could, Paul. If ... You Owned a Chrysler
★ Are You Getting It Every Day? (The *Sun*)
★ A Buck Well Spent On A Spring-Maid Sheet (A number that came complete with the visual of an exhausted Red Indian on a bed.)
★ What Makes A Shy Girl Get Intimate?
★ Should A Gentleman Offer A Tiparillo To A Lady?
★ The Beer That Made The Nineties Gay (Potosi Brewing Co, USA)
★ Is Your Wife Cold? (National Oil Fuel, USA)
★ Is Your Man Getting Enough? (Milk Marketing Board)
★ Give Him A Right Good Hemeling Tonight

* What's The Difference Between A Male Policeman And A Female Policeman? Six Inches (Police recruitment)
* Get Into Fellas (Fellas men's underwear, New Zealand)

Some US slogans are wonderfully mind-numbing:
* Do Away With Shaker Clog (International Salt Co., USA)
* Combines Fun With Manly Training (Daisy air rifle, USA)
* As Reliable As Grandfather's Clock And As Portable As The Cat (Perfection Oil Heaters, USA)

Some seem unbelievably self-defeating:
* Chase and Sanborn Coffee – It's Dated
* Dietz Lanterns – Safe As Sunshine (As any cancer specialist will tell you)

Others are perfect gems of the punster's art. Imagine all the work that went into the following snappy phrases before the company chairman was finally happy with what he'd written. Country of origin, again, USA:
* Best Glue In The Joint (Elmer's Glue)
* No Rust For The Wary (Dupont cooling system cleanser)
* One Good Ton Deserves Another (Doughtridge Fuel Co.)
* My Life Is An Open Look (Calox Tooth Powder)

One slogan, however, stands out above all. It is for Modart Fluff Shampoo:
* Does *your* hair sing when you rinse it?

OVERHEARD AT HEADHUNTER'S

'Nowadays, even mediocrity comes in pairs.'

OVERHEARD IN THE NEAL STREET RESTAURANT

'I never think six snails are enough, do you?'

. . . And Then There Were The Ones That Got Away

Every copywriter, on every account, has experienced that moment of sheer genius and insight when he dreams up a line which – if broadcast – would surely move nations. And every account man, on every account, has done his equal damnedest to ensure that the lines never saw the light of day. Until now . . .

★ Hail Jaffa, King Of The Juice

★ *For Brickwood's Beer:* Let The Sun Shine Out Of Your Glass

★ *For Playtex:* Her Cup Runneth Over

★ B-B-B-Butlins . . . Burgers, Booze 'n' Bonking

★ *For Panasonic, by Jerry Della Femina, who used it as the title for what was, until now, the world's best book of advertising:* From Those Wonderful Folks Who Gave You Pearl Harbor-

★ People Are Sticking To Kleenex

★ Carnation Milk is the best in the land;
Here I sit with a can in my hand –
No tits to pull, no hay to pitch,
You just punch a hole in the son of a bitch.

★ There was a young bridegroom called Pasco
Who anointed his tool with Tabasco;
The screams from his bride
As he thrust it inside
Made the first night a f***ing fiasco.

★ *For Pakistan International Airways:* Fly to Bangkok and Phuket

★ *For Kurt Geiger shoes:* Kurt Geiger Makes Women

★ *Rejected slogan for an American supermarket's own brand oil:* The only part of Popeye that doesn't rust is the part he puts in our Olive Oil

★ **** Curry – as recommended by Geoff Boycott: you still get the runs, but very slowly

★ *Rejected slogan for a pale ale called 'Time':* Peeing is a Waste of Time

★ *Rejected slogan for a market garden in Bath:* Kill a Tree For Christmas

★ *Rejected slogan for a chain of chemist shops:* Everything From Sunglasses For The Continent to Rubber Pants For The Incontinent

★ How does the Talbot Samba perform against the Porsche 911? Just fine. Now try getting laid because you own one.

★ *For a solid-fuel depot in Slough:* We're the biggest bunch of coke-sackers in town.

The all time greatest unused slogan? First among equals must be the writer on Tampax who in response to a competitor's tampon ad that had said: 'Modess . . . Because', wrote:

★ Tampax . . . Insofar As

And equally first: when Winston cigarettes ran a campaign that featured such strange visuals as a crowbar with a jam tart on top of it, with the line: We're Not Allowed To Tell You Anything About Winston Cigarettes So Here's A Tart Leaning On A Bar, the following suggestion was inexplicably rejected:

Visual: Shovel leaning against a wall, big rooster looking at it. Line: We're Not Allowed To Tell You Anything About Winston Cigarettes So Here's A Spade With A Giant Cock

Golden Turkey Award For The Worst Taste In Any Ad Ever, In Any Medium

Runner-up is a Chiswick motor company, for an ad with the headline: 'We've seen the light' over an illustration of Christ demonstrating a fleet of cars to a group of nodding disciples. The ad, apparently, was designed to tie in with the Christmas season.

But first prize, for what was surely the worst mail-shot of all time, goes to a London design group. Their mailer comprised four 3-inch nails, taped to a piece of white card, and bearing the legend: 'Do It Yourself Easter Kit.'

OVERHEARD AT LA CAPANNINA

'I don't think JWT is a gentleman's club any more. The board's a real cross-section these days – of Old Harrovians *and* Old Etonians . . .'

OVERHEARD IN PADDINGTON TRATTORIA

'Did you hear that Saatchi's almost bought Dorlands this week, until they discovered they already own it.'

OVERHEARD IN THE RITZ

'When it comes to restaurants I like La Coupole – although I can never decide which one, Park Avenue or Boulevard Montparnasse.'

Censored

So you've cracked the brief. You've written your ad or your script, and your worries are all over. Are they hell! You now have to run an obstacle course of blue pencils, wet blankets, and solid brick walls, starting with that old favourite, the account man. It is usually round about now that he decides he is employed by the client rather than by the agency, and tries his level best to second guess the ITCA, the ASA, the consumer, and just about everybody else who might have a pessimistic comment to make. But if you do manage to get your ad or script past him, you can now submit it to the official wet blankets.

The ITCA is in charge of vetting every single TV and radio script in an attempt to administer the IBA's Advertising Rules and Practices and in consequence save us from everything that isn't legal, decent, honest and truthful. ITCA stands for Inspiration Trampled, Caution Admired, Ideas That Committees Amend – or Independent Television Companies Association. It decrees that to protect the public you cannot depict a hangover in a script, only a 'headache with upset stomache'. You can't show children with bad table manners, and you certainly can't show a mirror over a fireplace, because that incites dangerous behaviour: people admiring themselves in the glass, while their clothes go up in flames. You can't have jingles in commercials about analgesics, and you can't have drinkers who look under the age of twenty-five. (When McEwan's did a commerical with an animated face on a can, the face had to be redrawn to look older.) Equally loony was their ruling on the script that opened on a salesman walking into a pub. The ITCA said that it would only be acceptable if the salesman was carrying a raincoat. Why? Apparently, all salesmen drive cars. You cannot imply that a character is drinking and driving – and a raincoat, ergo, would prove that the salesman was on foot.

Sometimes a commercial will slip through the ITCA net, only to be caught in the ITCA net: they also have the power to take ads off the air, even though they have previously been approved. A Heineken commerical featuring Nero and his thumb was banned after the ITCA received letters of complaint. According to the complainants, Heineken was making light of the slaughter of Christians.

Heineken also provides an excellent instance of how arbitrary the ITCA can be in its judgements. How can a body that disallows the word 'berk' to be used on air (because they reckon it's short for Berkeley Hunt, which is cockney rhyming slang for a part of the female anatomy), possibly allow a line as preposterous as 'Heineken refreshes the parts other beers cannot reach'?

It is interesting that the ITCA has no jurisdiction over the BBC. The two-minute commercial promoting the Beeb would never have been allowed on the other channel, for several reasons: Ronnie Corbett is seen smoking; John Cleese orders a double measure of spirits; Bob Geldof mentions a specific charity; sports personalities are associated with alcohol; and the pub setting has no natural connection with the advertiser's service in the first place.

Beating the ITCA can sometimes be half the fun of writing a script. The creative team who worked on Mateus Rosé wine a few years back managed to have a restaurant customer suggestively asking a pretty waitress: 'I suppose a duck's out of the question?' More recently, we have seen the erotic encounter between the girl in the Vivas commercial and a hand blowing machine – with everything being raised except the ITCA's eyebrows, it seems. And to cap it all, we had the consummate Skol commercial featuring mental arithmetic, with the male character working out that if he has a couple of cans himself he'll still 'be able to give Samantha one'.

There are encouraging signs of change, however. In a recent edition of *Television Register*, a summary of a coffee commercial explains that 'Diane Keen and her talking pussy have a bright start to the day with a lovely cup of Nescafé'. Can this possibly be construed as the start of a new enlightenment by our friends at 56 Mortimer Street?

Print advertising is regulated by the Advertising Standards Authority, under the chairmanship of 65-year-old Lord McGregor of Durris and his personally selected 12-man council. It is one of the most influential jobs in the country, because their taste dictates what the rest of us see – or don't see – printed as ads in newspapers, magazines, posters or books. What are his views on sex in advertising? Feminists will be pleased to know that Lord McGregor was quoted in the *Mail on Sunday* as saying: 'What we are talking about is fantasy. Life would be intolerable without it ... I told [the Women's Media Action Group] last week that my fantasy was strapping a diamond to a beautiful gel's thigh ... Sexual to me means intercourse. Sexual fantasies are unrelated to that.'

One can't help feeling sometimes what a great pity it is that our own controls are not as liberal as those in Singapore. There, 'Kwan Loong Double Lion Medicated Oil' is allowed to advertise itself as 'The Trusted One', giving effective relief from 'headaches, stuffy nose, stomach flatulence, muscular pains, giddiness and insect bites'. The pack goes on to claim that The Trusted One also heals 'bruises, cuts, sprains, dislocations, fainting fits, colds, coughs, cramps and toothache, and helps prevent influenza and contagious diseases'.

Meanwhile, back at the agency, if the account man and the ITCA both approve your script, it can now be presented to the client. And if he says yes, the idea will then go into research.

OVERHEARD AT AGENCY INTERVIEW

'My dear chap, advertising culture is a contradiction in terms.'

OVERHEARD AFTER CLIENT MEETING

'That guy is bilingual. He speaks English and bullshit.'

'If Everything in Life Serves a Useful Purpose, How Come Market Researchers?'

Creatives are never sure why research is done at all. After all, some of the best campaigns in history researched so badly that it was only because the client loved the idea and was brave enough to defend it that the advertising ever ran. Heineken, again, is a good example: research killed the 'refreshes the parts' idea stone dead, but Frank Lowe loved it, the client loved it, and they insisted that the campaign ran regardless. The surreal Benson & Hedges campaign was never even tested – on the grounds that the advertising was so different from anything ever done before that the public would not know how to react to it. (Isn't all advertising supposed to be like that?)

It would be churlish and unprofessional, however, to suggest that research is totally without detectable use. It is often able to supply penetrating insights into consumer behaviour, as the following paragraph from a research document ably demonstrates: 'The swallowing and the continuance of the flavour are important aspects of toffee and help to differentiate it from items like chewing-gum, which, although they involve the chewing activity, offer quite different gratifications. The climax of eating a toffee is the reduction of the size of the sweet by an ever-increasing rate of chewing until the residue can be ingested. There seem to be sexual parallels and we believe that toffee-eating might act as an oral equivalent of genital sex, involving effort, rhythm and a quality of compulsive acceleration.' Thanks, chaps. They say that feeling guided and directed is the start of creativity.

Well, if your script passes all the hurdles, you can now go

into production. Your choice of director will obviously depend on what you know about his choice of restaurants, but from then on you can leave everything in his capable hands. All you have to worry about is what time you want the limo to come and pick you up from home on each day of shooting, and whether to have an egg and bacon roll, or a sausage and bacon roll, or both (depends where you're booked into for lunch), when the breakfast trolley is wheeled onto the set at 10. You'll then have a few days of standing around to put up with, watching over-paid technicians on the over-manned set put your film together for you, followed by an arduous couple of weeks of walking to Soho several times a day on post-production matters and claiming for cabs, meals and refreshments. But then Bob's your uncle. You're a star. And it's going to cost the agency another ten grand a year if they want you to stay.

OVERHEARD IN L.A.

'There must be thousands of rats in Madison Avenue. Of course, I am only speaking from memory.'

OVERHEARD AT PHOTOGRAPHER'S PARTY

'I know an account exec who's so stupid, all the other account execs have noticed.'

OVERHEARD IN ACCOUNT EXEC'S OFFICE

'What's all the fuss about? It's going to be fish and chip paper tomorrow.'

How To Be a Client

When the Client moans and sighs
Make his logo twice the size.
If he still should prove refractory,
Show a picture of his factory.
Only in the gravest cases
Should you show the clients' faces

Not so very long ago, a small but ambitious West End agency was about to pitch for a new client. The presentation was arranged for 11 o'clock in the morning, the boardroom was ready, the coffee was perking. At precisely 10.50 a member of the agency team suddenly clutched his chest and fell to the ground, stone dead. He'd had a heart attack. Seconds later, the telephone went. It was the receptionist: the prospective new client had arrived, and was waiting downstairs. With commendable concern for the welfare of those members of the agency who still needed to earn a living, the team did the only thing they could in the circumstances. They shoved the body into a cupboard in the corner of the room and carried on with the presentation. The agency won the business, and rushed their new client out to lunch to celebrate – pausing only to ask the receptionist discreetly to call an ambulance.

The story is not far-fetched. Agencies will move heaven and earth to win business and keep clients happy. A director of one of the top agencies used to have trouble getting out of bed in the morning (even when it was his own). His agency won a northern client whose train got into Euston at 9 o'clock, meaning that the client could be in the agency for a meeting by 9.30. The account director's solution was to send the agency limousine to meet him every time; unbeknown to the client, the chauffeur then took in most of London on the journey, complaining about the traffic all the way and reaching the agency dead on 10am. This went on for about a year, until a new director took over the piece of business and was so horrified by what had been happening that he told the chauffeur to take a more direct route. The driver complied, but was bright enough to improve the journey time by only a little each week, explaining that he was at last finding new and better ways of beating the traffic. The client was none the wiser.

Becoming a client can seriously damage your liver. Your life will be one long lunch. And dinner, if you ask for it, with theatre and a late-night drinking club to follow. No wonder provincial agencies find it so hard to pitch against London agencies: why would a client want a day out in the agency down the road when he could be whooping it up in the agency in London – with an overnight stop because he's working so late?

To help you be a better client, here are a few rules.

1. Love your product, but not so much that you'll mind not seeing it in the ads the junior team knocked out ten minutes before you left for the restaurant.

2. Be aware that you can get through much more business during a three-hour session at the White Tower than during a one-hour working lunch back at base.

3. Be delighted that your opposite number at the agency enjoys a far more glamorous lifestyle than you do. Be pleased that he enjoys a smartly located office, plush decor, pretty receptionists and day-long lunch hours.

4. Never say thank you, you'll arouse suspicion. Better to praise endlessly work by the agency's competitors, to give you an edge.

5. Carry a copy of *Ogilvy On Advertising*, and quote from it often.

6. Insist that your wife's opinion carry as much weight as your own.

7. Do not be open-minded – agencies like bastards they can pigeon-hole.

We Should Be Talking To Each Other

Advertising agencies have the skills to change people's attitudes to the point where they function in a prescribed fashion. So said Vance Packard in *The Hidden Persuaders*, and in no area of their operations do agencies have more persuasive skills than when it comes to pitches.

Creative pitches are the presentation of tentative advertising campaigns in the hope of winning accounts, when agencies stage spectaculars that put Spielberg to shame.

Speculative pitches are expensive. They cost from £25,000 to £150,000. With that many sovs at stake, it's no wonder that dignity goes out of the window. An agency as intellectual as Boase Massimi Pollitt dressed up in yellow pages' uniforms to pitch for the Yellow Pages account. The chairman and vice-chairman of another major agency took temporary jobs behind the counter at Kentucky Fried Chicken when they were trying for the business.

Agencies will go to great lengths to win pitches. When JWT was pitching for British Rail, they mobilised practically the whole agency of 500 people. Everyone who travelled to work by train had to fill in questionnaires by the dozen, and the use of company cars was banned for a week to encourage further research. Some employees were less faithful to the edict than others. A creative director went to a meeting in Manchester by train, but came back by air. This, he explained, was so that he could make an accurate comparison of the two modes of transport.

One of the nicest aspects of pitching is winning. Then the

51

champagne flows as if it were Friday afternoon, and there's a rush to put expenses through while the agency's still in euphoric mode. Boase Massimi Pollitt celebrate their wins in characteristically witty fashion. When they heard that they had won the £2 million pound Royal Bank of Scotland and William and Glyn's account, they sent an internal memo to all employees. Stapled to the tidings was a genuine Royal Bank of Scotland £1 note. 'At last,' the message read. 'A client who makes something really useful.'

So what is it like to be a prospective client on the receiving end of all this agency enthusiasm, effort, and attention? What can you expect to happen to you after your initial approach to them to say that you'd like them to pitch?

Within three or four days of the first contact (sooner looks rather ill-prepared, later and another agency will have stolen their march), a team of three or four agency people (more and you'd consider them overpowering, less and you'd consider it insulting) will descend on you to ask intelligent questions that will impress you. They will tour your factory if you have one, and get out into the field and talk to your salesmen (in the hope that word will get back to you about how keen they are). The director in charge of the pitch will send you thank-you letters after each meeting, together with a mailing piece that tells you everything you always wanted to know about the agency but were too afraid of being bored to ask. The aim is to establish some sort of rapport within seven days.

Back at the agency, the planner will have been set loose on The Brief, the creative team will be beavering away on The Solution, and the account handlers will be writing The Immaculate Document. Within two weeks of your first contact, and with just one week to go, they will be starting rehearsals. They may even have hired a presentations director, who will orchestrate the whole proceedings. He will time the performers, brush up their delivery, suggest link themes, suggest ways of dramatising arguments, assess potential audience reaction. The agency will have rehearsed its 90-minute presentation (that's the norm) several times before you see them, including two full dress rehearsals. Both of the jokes (that's the norm, too) will have been honed to perfection; not a single ad lib will be out of place.

On presentation day, you will arrive at the agency to be greeted by a trail of giant bear footprints (if your account is

Brown Bear) or a giant inflatable McDonald's arch around the agency's main entrance (if your account is McDonald's).

The agency will seat you at a table if they can – it's more intimate. If there are a lot of people, you will be seated in a horseshoe, thus allowing presenters to move closer to you. The principal presenter will occupy the head of the table, and the agency chairman or managing director will probably be seated amongst your team. This imparts a degree of implied intimacy, and prevents you from passing notes.

The agency will field the least number of people who can act as a team. (Only later will you come across the skilful man-to-man marking that makes agencies such brilliant manipulators.) Now never mind how, but the agency will know the personal history of each and every one of you, your temperament, your rank and your likely views, and they will have isolated decision makers and potential trouble makers well in advance.

The agency will start by revealing the rationale and proposed strategy. This will be over and done with as quickly as possible, because they know you'll switch off if you don't see creative work within twenty minutes. JWT are masters of the rationale reveal. To illustrate how dull Weetabix are in comparison to Kellogg's Corn Flakes, the Sunshine Breakfast, they presented the clients with a pair of slippers in a cereal bowl.

We now have the Theme Reveal, and the creative work is wheeled on. Or rather, electric curtains part to reveal it, people jump out of cakes or parachute down from the ceiling with it, or the presenters may even stand up and sing it to you. Jingles will boom, films will run. Questions will then be invited, and you will be cajoled into staying for lunch. If you're the chairman of ICI and you want to disarm them, you'll nod and say: 'Thanks, I'll have a cheese and pickle on white, and a tin of Fanta.'

OVERHEARD IN RECEPTION

'We've got fifteen balls in the air on this project, and two of them are mine.'

An Arm and a Leg: The Anatomy of a Shoot

All shoots are the same, it's just that for some of them you wear your Bermudans, and for those at Shepperton or Pinewood you don't. Whatever the location, your main responsibility as an agency person is to arrive on the set at about nine-ish – to check what progress the director and crew have made since they started at six, and to give them the benefit of any creative input you may like to make. You then need to watch them at work until the stroke of ten, when the breakfast trolley arrives laden with bacon rolls, bacon and sausage rolls, egg rolls, egg and bacon rolls, egg and sausage rolls, tea and coffee. Then there's rather a long haul to lunch time, filled usually by snooping around other people's sets on adjoining stages, or chatting to the make-up person, the continuity person, the assistant director, the second assistant director, the floor manager, the focus puller, the clapper loader, the camera and crane grip/rigger driver, the lighting cameraman/lighting director, the camera operator, the sound crew, the hairdresser, the carpenters, the electricians, the wardrobe person, the plasterers, the plumbers, the stagehands, the stills cameraman, the prop man, the scene painters, the set designer, the home economist, the vision mixer or any of the 127 people so indispensable to the shoot. But never actors or actresses: all they want to talk about is left-wing politics, and however grateful they are for being cast, they certainly won't put out for agency wallies. They save that for the clapper loader or crane driver.

The only member missing at this stage from what directors

lovingly call the 'armchair brigade' is the client. He will arrive at about ten to one, do a quick mental head count, and ask a loaded question about the re-making of *Ben Hur*. If you still fail to recognise him after this, he's the one with the tears falling down from one end of his body (onto the sixteen very expensive sections, in six foolscap pages, of the production company's estimate) and with the account man's face firmly implanted up the other.

At last, it's lunch – and the chance to exchange a word or two with the director. Words like 'Gosh, I didn't know Cellnet worked in restaurants, it must be marvellous to be able to sit here and arrange next week's assignment with Milan direct'. And then, sadly, it's back to the set.

J. Walter Thompson has a reputation for producing commercials that are very high on the 'aah factor' – that is, they star lots of lovely cuddly animals, and viewers go 'aah' a lot when they see them. A year or two ago, Bowater-Scott, a JWT client, wanted four new commercials for Andrex. Based on the four seasons of the year, the commercials were designed to show the Andrex puppy playing with other lovely little animals, thereby raising the 'aah factor' associated with the brand. It was a fairly typical shoot.

Naturally, because of the vagaries of the English weather, it was decided to film 'Spring' (in which the puppy plays with a sweet little bunny rabbit) and 'Autumn' (in which he plays with a cute little squirrel), in California. An English country scene would then be built on location.

The film crew consisted of thirty-five people, twenty-five Andrex puppies (each between six and eight weeks old), 200 fake daffodils, 2,000 brown plastic leaves and thirty odd cases of Andrex toilet tissue. The team arrived in California to find that it was raining. Contrary to all the rules of west coast weather, it then continued to rain for a further three days. The location site was flooded. Then one of the trucks, carrying members of the film crew, was involved in a road accident. And a tree fell on another one.

Then one of the animal trainers failed to show up. His wife had shot him. And when that little problem was solved, there was a new development on the dog front. Puppies get tired very quickly under powerful studio lights, which is why it takes so many of them to make a single 30-second commercial. (To save confusion, the trainers mark on the bottom of their paws which ones have already been used, and which are better at doing certain things.)

But when filming finally got under way, it was also discovered that Andrex puppies and sweet little bunnies really aren't a good mix. The dogs try to eat the rabbits, and the rabbits try to make themselves very scarce. It took a lot of film, and an awful lot of patience, before the requisite scenes had been shot. And then, as the teams moved on to 'Autumn', they discovered that Andrex puppies and cute little squirrels aren't such a good mix either.

Photographic shoots are very much the same as film shoots, it's just that there are 127 fewer people standing around discussing their overtime rates. One particular shoot, for the British Telecom 'Make that call' campaign, is a fair example. Most clients insist on a strict 'no willies' rule when animals are on camera, and this was the shoot where nobody remembered to remind the actors . . .

The poster was to show a sheepdog on the phone, 'rounding up' his friends. The photographer had therefore ordered a stuffed paw with a telephone glued on the end, plus two live sheepdogs – one to be photographed, and one as a spare. The agency supplying the animals interpreted this as meaning that one of the sheepdogs was to be a dog and the other a bitch, which wouldn't have mattered in the slightest, had the bitch not been on heat.

At the start of the session both animals were in the studio together, but it soon became obvious that the bitch was far more interested in being mounted by her friend than in posing for the camera. In the end, the agency art director decided to lock the dog in his car outside. So out he went with the dog, much to the frustration of the bitch, which immediately started to feel nervous. The art director, meanwhile, thought it would make sense to kill two birds with one stone by retrieving the stuffed paw from the photographer's car . . .

As far as the bitch was concerned, the man had taken her mate outside because he was cross with him. Now he had returned, and there was a severed leg in his hand. She took one look and was off. More than an hour later, the photographer, the photographer's assistant and the agency art director were still trying to coax the poor, trembling girl down from her perch – the studio lighting gantries some twenty feet above their heads.

We're Talking Telephone Number Salaries . . .

Mike Yershon was taken to breakfast a few years ago by an executive from Leo Burnett. The events of that meeting were to become an advertising legend. Yershon had just quit his post as media director at Collett Dickenson Pearce to set up his own business. He was not looking for a job – but Burnett's wanted him. At the end of the meeting, so the story goes, the man from Burnett's reached into his briefcase, pulled out a blank cheque, and invited his guest to name his price. To his eternal credit, do you know what Yershon did? That's right, he joined Burnett's.

Such inducements are still rife. A creative director of a big agency not a million miles from Berkeley Square was sitting in his office one day when one of his most talented copywriters, who had been with the agency for thirteen years, came in and tendered his resignation. The creative director went right through the standard A-Z Of Bribes in a justifiable – but futile – attempt to make the copywriter stay. In the end, he wheeled out the company chequebook and did a Burnett's. Perhaps because he thought the Yershon tactic was old hat, the copywriter declined. When last seen, he looked miserable. Perhaps he'd realised too late the truth of the old advertising maxim: Money isn't everything, it's the *only* thing.

Nobody in advertising is on the breadline. Most people pull very nice bucks indeed. That's because good creative talent is in short supply, and in any case, advertising people work about three times as hard as anybody else in British industry. (Check the position of 'Copywriter' in the list of stressful jobs: it comes a close second, just behind 'Prime Minister'.)

Some people do really very nicely, and the word 'Seymour' was coined as a unit of currency in 1983 when Geoff Seymour was lured away from Lowe Howard-Spink to be made a creative director at Saatchi and Saachi for a reported salary of £100,000. From that moment, it was fashionable to quote salaries in fractions of the name. Or even multiples: Don White went from Benton and Bowles to McCann-Erickson soon afterwards as creative director for a salary reputedly not unadjacent to 1.2 Seymours.

When it comes to money, advertising is the perfect example of a free market operating under the laws of supply and demand: everyone negotiates their own salary individually. Hardly surprising, you might say, in any industry that believes in market forces, let alone one that survives on them. But the laws of supply and demand alone do not explain why the bigger agencies have found themselves forking out increasingly large packages in the last few years. The market forces are distorted by many factors peculiar to advertising.

For a start, it's the creative department that comes up with the ideas which keep the agency in business, so the creative department must be very well rewarded. Unfortunately they're so well rewarded that most top creatives can afford not to have to stick around much after the age of forty or so – unless they have the right sort of carrots dangled in front of them.

Few agencies train people up from scratch any more. An agency that takes on trainees will have them half-inched before they can fulfil their promise – so why bother? This problem was compounded by general recruitment cuts in the mid-seventies' recession, which has in turn created a large generation gap in most creative departments. The only remedy is to poach ready-made staff, and it's a remedy that agencies are having to pay through the nose for.

Headhunters must also share the blame for the salary eruption (or the credit, depending on which side of the interview you're sitting). There are four or five companies operating solely in the advertising field, and they all charge 15 per cent of the first year's salary for successful placements. It is obviously in their interest to see that salaries are pushed ever higher: an agency using their services to find a senior creative team is likely to end up with a bill that leaves very little change out of £20,000.

So exactly how much *do* advertising people earn? Getting an adman to reveal details of his salary package is like trying to break into a safe with a stick of rhubarb. And don't tell the Advertising Standards Association this, but admen also tend to lie a little bit . . .

The *Tatler* listed three admen in a feature on Britain's highest earners. Peter Marsh, one of the founding partners of Allen Brady Marsh, was scraping along on £305,000. Jeremy Pemberton, creative director of Yellowhammer, was also on the list, and of course good creative directors, as we know, don't come cheaper than a Seymour.

A senior copywriter or art director these days might command a package worth £65,000 – £75,000, consisting of a £45,000 basic salary and a wheelbarrow-load of perks (we'll come on to those in a minute). Junior teams can expect about £15,000, and starters about half that. Good planners earn about £30,000, good media directors about £30,000 – £40,000. Account directors earn about the same or more. The average account executive gets about £20,000 or less. Agency chairmen deserve less still, and are of course paid even more – the highest salaries being at agencies which offer no equity slice, like the multinationals, where the average earns in the region of £100,000 – £150,000.

OVERHEARD IN ACCOUNT DIRECTOR'S OFFICE

RESIGNING EXEC TO DIRECTOR: 'The reason I want to move on is because I feel I'm not learning anything.'

ACCOUNT DIRECTOR: 'But my dear boy, you don't understand. There isn't anything to learn . . .'

. . . And A Porsche

Your basic salary in advertising is, of course, just the beginning. Perks and benefits then shovel about a foot of icing onto an already rich cake. Perhaps not to the extreme of some directors, who have been known to claim in their company annual reports that they draw no salary at all, but instead put everything from cigarettes to lavatory paper through on company expenses. But there's no doubt that if you can eat, drink, travel, clothe yourself and generally live off the agency, you'll find it a most congenial place to be.

The fringe benefits start, as you would suspect, with a company car. Or two. (As one agency chairman is reputed to have told a copywriter he very much wanted to keep: 'You can have anything you want down there in the car park, except the Ferrari – that's mine.')

AT 60 MILES AN HOUR THE LOUDEST NOISE IN AN ADMAN'S CAR COMES FROM THE RACAL VODAPHONE

In advertising, you are what you drive, and what you drive is not actually always a Porsche. It all depends on who your headhunter is. Some have got so used to negotiating the standard package that you'll end up with the usual BMW or gleaming white convertible Golf GTi whether you like it or not.

But a Porsche of some sort or another is still what most adpeople need to get them from A to B – or rather, from the Agency to the Zanzibar.

There are signs, however, that the climate is changing. One multi-award-winning art director – ever a reliable barometer of what's occurring on the car front – has eased off a little from his Porsche, Ferrari and Corvette days, and is settling down happily with a little Alfa Spider. It seems that the more awards a person wins – and the higher therefore their worth when it comes to their next move – the more likely they are to venture off the beaten status symbol track. E-type Jags are now double-parking outside the Zanzibar along with the best of them, driven by art directors too young to have heard of Simon Dee; so, too, are 1956 Panhard Dynas, Pontiac Firebirds, and the odd 1948 Studebaker pick-up or two. Not a Montego in sight, though. Could it be that the boys at Burnett's don't believe their own propaganda?

Then there's petrol, of course, removal expenses, a pension plan, cheap loans, health care, a generous entertainment allowance, and a free TV and video – all fairly standard bolt-ons these days. There can also be some rather more exotic perks, depending on your powers of negotiation: perhaps unlimited free groceries, almost unquestioned use of credit cards, a company flat up in town, use of a company villa in the sun, private education for your kids – you name it. A seat on the board, profit-sharing and share option schemes are also increasingly popular benefits these days.

A delightful new practice whose roots can be traced back to Yershon's famous breakfast is the concept of a non-refundable transfer fee, or 'golden hello'. Basically it's a one-off payment – sometimes as much as £50,000 – which the player can keep even if he decides to stay at his present agency and not move after all. (Except that he'd be likely to find any future movement somewhat difficult, on two broken legs.) Holidays are also a good wheeze, and one creative director is famous for adding one extra week's holiday to his demands each time he changes agencies. At the last count, he was on eight weeks' annual paid holiday.

The Advertising Cost of Living Index

Advertising salaries – why have they risen so fast? Tests now prove that nine out of ten salaries have grown in 100 per cent direct correlation with the purchase price trend of the following essential advertising items:

A Sony Walkman
A Zippo lighter
A Porsche 928S
A pair of Raybans
A Mont Blanc pen
A Tizio anglepoise
A pair of Cutler and Gross spectacles
A Filofax
An American yellow writing-pad
A pack of Camel or Marlboro
A silvery metal camera-case-type briefcase
A Paul Smith suit and bow tie
A pair of Levi 501s
A pair of Brooks boots
A gramme of coke
A Hi-Tec converted warehouse in Limehouse
A bottle of Krug
A Braun designer stubble trimmer

'Show Me A Man's Designer Stubble And I'll Tell You The Story Of His Life'

'Only fools don't judge by appearances,' said Oscar Wilde, award-winning creative of a few years back – and the boy was right. From the adman's point of view, if you can't pigeon-hole your target audience on sight, how on earth can you start flogging them something at once? Adfolk have taken the principle so much to heart that they've made sure they themselves can be instantly labelled. Designer labelled, at that.

Among the agency admin staff for example you'll always find the chairman in his club tie, New & Lingwood shirt, and Gieves and Hawkes chalkstripe (all chosen with the help of a Douglas Sutherland book on how to be a gentleman). Then there's the media man in his Tommy Nutter foreign exchange dealer suit from Austin Reed, know what I mean John, got time for another swift half? The account exec, in either a Paul Smith, Reiss, or Woodhouse number if he works at a trendy agency; or, if he's at JWT, whatever the MD was wearing the day before, except with a briefcase. That just leaves the account director. He's always dressed, sincerely and successfully, in either gold Amex or platinum Diners – or both. Adwomen, whatever their position in the heirarchy, always wear clothes that are both sexy and practical – exciting to look at, yet without any frills or floppy bits that might get in the way while they're pouring the coffee.

As we get closer to the engine room we find the account planners, shuffling around like out-of-work extras from *Goodbye, Mr Chips* in faithful suits or baggy, patterned sweaters, tweed jackets and cords. Lift up the designer rumpled hair though and you'll invariably find a tiny earring – believed to be an acupuncture device to keep them awake whilst listening to market researchers.

That just leaves us with the TV department before we get to the coal-face proper. It's often hard to tell the difference between a TV producer and a creative director, especially after a few glasses of champagne in the Martinez bar in Cannes. All-over beards are quite important with this lot, nestling below a pair of whacky red or green specs from Cutler and Gross. Then it's the striped cotton preppy jacket (a nice bit of classic Americana: shows you do the States a lot), and either grey flannels with pastel Argyll socks and loafers or designer jeans with solid Fabian fellwalkers or Grenson brogues. Accessories to match include a brushed aluminium camera-case-style briefcase, and a green leather Filofax.

OK, now here we are in the creative department, in amongst the workers. It's easy to spot an art director, even from the other end of the aperitif bar at Langan's. They're the ones with highlights and Ian Botham hairdos, and dressed in crumpled designer suits with every crease immaculately art directed to create the perfect casual effect. Or maybe they've got the rather severe fifties jazz musician barnet number, plus leather jacket, T-shirt and Levis. Either way, they'll also be wearing American Brooks boots (broad white sports shoes punched with air-holes) or classic brown brogues.

And now a word about designer stubble. Menopausal creative directors have gone for the Nicholson/Hoffman/Pacino/De Niro/Charles Dance type of look for a year or two now. Many senior art directors (and one or two senior writers with identity crises) have opted more for the George Michael/Don Johnson/Martin Kemp/Bob Geldof-type effect. Junior art directors haven't started shaving yet.

Few secretaries have designer stubble. They achieve *their* effect at Pacific in Mayfair's South Molton Street, or at Top Shop, Chelsea Girl or Che Guevara. And the effect is always explosively sexy, with tight jeans, or mini-skirts, or T-shirts, all carefully chosen to show off the parts of their anatomy that got them their jobs in the first place.

Writers? They all look like unmade beds. Or as though they've dunked their bodies in Superglue and hurled them-selves through the window of an Oxfam shop.

This Chapter Degrades Women

'Advertising is the most fun you can have with your clothes on,' a famous adman once said. That was back in the good old days before we had wimmin up in arms about such innocuous headlines as Hoover's 'Who's built a turbo for women drivers?' or Epson Computers' 'So simple your mother could use it'. The days when, to quote a recent film poster, 'Women were women and men were animals'. The only way you can have as much fun in an agency nowadays is by staying late at the office and piling your clothes neatly on the floor next to your secretary's.

This chapter is all about staying late at the office, or as we call it in advertising, 'sex'. It's about sex in advertising, and sex in advertising agencies. The two go hand in hand, linked as inextricably as a pissed account director and an ambitious PA. If advertising has anything to do with real life, then sex will always have something to do with advertising.

A few years ago, researchers from the Strathclyde Business School carried out the first ever survey into love at work. They concluded that the diversion of energy into office sex was seriously undermining the country's industrial performance. What a pity they never went near an ad agency. They might have learned that far from doing any harm, a little of what you fancy does no end of creative good.

Of the 15,000 people who work in advertising, roughly half are women. But it's a very bottom-heavy pyramid. Most of them are telephonists, receptionists, accounts clerks, tea-ladies, bar staff (all the bigger agencies have their own in-house pubs or wine bars), shop staff (they have their own in-house mini supermarkets, too), PAs or secretaries. Of the remaining few per cent of women you'll find one or two creatives, slightly greater numbers of account handlers, and a positive skew of planners. That's because an advertising agency is simply a microcosm of the real world: those who can, do; those who can't, take the client to lunch. And while that's going on, *someone* has to stay behind and look after the house.

Women at the beginning of the century were slaves of the kitchen and nursery and swathed in long dresses – but the power of advertising has liberated them from all that. First there were ads that broke new ground with a glimpse of stocking. Later, the full-blown leg crept onto the hoardings, invariably doing the Charleston. Then when the market for shoes and stockings was saturated, the advertisers moved slowly up the female body, emancipating as they went. One by one, all the old Victorian no-go areas were de-odorised, de-haired, up-lifted, shown off.

By the time TV advertising got into its stride in the late fifties, it had shaped the totally modern woman of today. Stepford Wives with heads full of soap, unable to tell Stork from butter, but fully equipped to join Jimmy Young in strenuous debates about Ariel versus the boil wash. Wives with cookability and the glow of fulfilment known only to those who keep their adoring nuclear families in sunshine breakfasts and clothes that are Persil white and free from the stains we prefer not to talk about. Women who sing songs to their truck driver sons about being chums with their gums, and who know that the way to a man's heart is through a slogan. Above all, women who are germ-fighters, standing bravely between their families and the certain death that awaits them from the 99.9 per cent of all known household germs that are lying in wait under the lavvie seat.

Not content with this, market researchers are always trying to help find new 'segments' of consumers for advertisers to exploit. A 'Woman Study' published by McCann-Erickson grouped women into the categories of The Avant Guardian, The Lady Righteous, The Hopeful Seeker, The Lack-A-Daisy, The Lively Lady, The New Unromantic, The Blinkered and The Down-Trodden. They needn't have bothered. To the real decision-makers in an advertising agency, female consumers are what they have always been. The ones that dance backwards. The ones that buy products featured in '2CK' commercials – '2 Characters in a Kitchen' (although the shorthand is normally used in a rather more explicit reference to the female anatomy).

Yes, baby, you've come a long way. So doesn't advertising deserve a little vote of thanks for the leg-up it's given you? Remember, we've always pressed for equal rights for women. The fact that this is interpreted by the ungrateful as an equal right to develop cancer of the lung or cirrhosis of the liver is neither here nor there.

How does this attitude affect life within the advertising agency? Not at all, is the answer. Women are still allowed to sleep their way to the top. 'I got my first job in advertising because I've got jolly big tits,' says one pragmatic, and highly successful, female copywriter.

The only fly in the ointment is that clients tend not to like women. Brewers and Japanese companies tend not to like them very much at all. Bits o' fluff undermine the 'pint in the pub' aspects of the business they say. Husbands don't like their wives being in advertising very much, either. The job demands a fair quota of 14-hour stints of toil and extra-curricular socialising. Few husbands will stand for their wives arriving home in the small hours complaining of sore feet (or a sore back).

Such hiccups apart, all ad agencies live and breathe sex. Even the terminology is sex-based: people handle accounts; service clients; pitch for sexy accounts; write ballsy copy that's strong on penetration.

Agencies love the chance to go to castings where they can spend a whole day inspecting the most beautiful meat in Britain – and later spend a whole day photographing it, with moody lighting, chilled Chablis, and little mirrors with lines of powder on them.

Given the choice between all this and your own working day, wouldn't you rather be Hemeling, too?

'Now is the Time for all Good Admen to come to the Aid of the Party'

Newly arrived? Newly married? Just got pregnant? Just got divorced? Just got a P45?

Not a day goes by, not a single personal landmark is allowed to pass, that isn't commemorated by someone, somewhere in the agency with the happy sound of a twenty-one-cork salute. Adpeople are party people. Adland is partyland; if you can't stand the heat, get out of the drinks cabinet.

Whatever the occasion, management is always happy to pick up the tab. It's their way of working off guilt – because they know that you know that the new arrival has come in on 65 and a Merc, because they've just fired you, or worse, because they're refusing to pay last month's expenses. They pick up the most lavish tabs at leaving parties. They know how vulnerable you feel all of a sudden (doesn't matter whether the person leaving jumped or whether they were pushed, the feeling's the same). Add champagne, and you're left feeling just plain off your guard. Now's the moment when they take you to one side and tell you the latest changes in your own working arrangements – a new partner perhaps, a new office . . . or a new P45.

Certain agencies go large on certain events. One of them used to be very big on fortieth birthdays. One week before his big occasion, the vice chairman was told by his managing director that the agency was pitching for the Portuguese Tourist Board account, and that the two of them would have to go to Portugal at once to do a factory visit. The vice chairman was met at Heathrow by his wife in disguise, and whisked off for a few days at a tennis ranch on the Algarve, courtesy of the agency. On his return to London, his actual birthday was celebrated in grand style. There was a party at the office, and after the first few cases of Moët had been demolished the guests were decanted into a coach that took them to the ground of his home team. The agency sponsored the game that night, and after a champagne reception the vice chairman received an autographed ball. He was reported to be over the moon.

Where and how to hold the Christmas party? Shall we have it on our own premises? Or shall we go and wreck somebody else's? (Never mention the word 'Saatchi' at the Hippodrome.) These are the decisions that in even the biggest agency are taken right up at boardroom level.

JWT take over the Savoy and splash out a few bob on special decor and the odd Jimmy Tarbuck or two. Saatchis, well, just never mention the Hippodrome. McCann's threw a real biggie in its own building in 1983. The party was so loud that the noise penetrated the nearby studios of Capital Radio, who talked about it on the air. Each member of staff had received a square of red carpet as an invitation, on which was printed: 'The kind of treatment you can expect on 1st December.'

The occasion certainly lived up to its promise: according to reports on Capital Radio, the last guest was dragged kicking and screaming from the building at 6am. But then, they couldn't see the back door.

Virgin Atlantic's new agency pushed the flying-boat out by holding their Christmas party in New York. Staff were flown out on their client's airline, and succeeded in drinking the galleys dry by mid-flight. On the return trip, the agency's head of art did a full strip-tease in the snooty Upper Class cabin. His colleagues contented themselves with drinking the galleys dry by mid-flight.

No wonder one of the first questions you ask when an agency is trying to poach you is: 'What did you do for your Christmas party last year?'

OVERHEARD IN THE WHITE TOWER

'I lent my agency to someone and they broke it.'

Award Yourself The C.D.M.

In the olden days (sort of 1970s), the way to enhance your reputation (and, in turn, your salary) was to chuck your typewriter out of the fifth floor window. But with the advent of double-glazing and the rising cost of typewriters, this laudable practice became increasingly difficult and expensive. New means of self-advertising had to be found and the trade papers leapt eagerly into the breach. All you have to do nowadays is whizz down to the Zanzibar, Filofax in hand (at Moscow's you can leave it on the special Filofax ledge they've provided under each table), and talk at great length about which £1,000-a-day photographer you've been working with. The gossip columnists will do all the rest – though it must be a nightmare for them in the rush hour (7.00pm – midnight), when all the stars are trying to make themselves heard at once above the steady background rumble of exploding champagne corks.

Creatives used to ask: Is this ad on strategy? Does it have a future? Will it flog widgets? But now the only question is: How will it look in my book? Or rather: Is it what the judges will be looking for? Some people will do anything to win prizes.

No other industry, not even the film industry, gets together quite as often as adfolk do to clap themselves on the back. Awards are the only reasonable measure of the quality of one's work, the argument goes. And because good advertising gives the client more for his pound than the mediocre kind, it makes good commercial sense for him to go where the creativity is. No wonder so many agencies are caught up in the mad awards scramble. To see what all the fuss is about, let's don our Ellesse

70

beachwear and Raybans and head down to the south of France. 'Awards are hell,' said the late Peter Finch, 'unless awarded to oneself.' He's obviously never been down to press the flesh at the International Advertising Film Festival in Cannes – the most award-winning awards ceremony of them all, the week in June, according to one creative director, 'when people say to your face what for 51 weeks they've been saying behind your back'.

As far as clients are ever told, you've gone to the festival to see hundreds of commercials from all over the world, meet the people who made them, then discuss ways and means of making them more cheaply. The Germans and the Japanese are down at the Palais du Congres all the time earnestly watching the screen, the Americans are busy getting quotes from each other for *Advertising Age*, and the Italians are holding funny cocktail parties in their own language. The Brits are far more conscientious, spending their time strolling along La Croisette from the Majestic to the Martinez, meeting each other at their set bars, pools or beaches in order to discuss business.

Most of the humour at Cannes stems from prices, in fact. A few years ago, a company came up with the idea of filming the reaction of the British contingent to the price of a cup of coffee. Cameras were hidden at one of the cabanas on the Plage Sportif, and a barman was persuaded to charge the first English person to come in an astronomical sum. The anticipated fracas never occurred. The punter paid up like a lamb – after all, it *was* agency money. This despite the fact that the barman charged the first person £10 for a single cup of coffee, the second £15, and so on up, by increments of £5, until someone willingly parted with an unbelievable £40.

It's not just the money that's ludicrous at Cannes. So are some of the 2,000 or so comercials that are presented. Here is a little sample. From Japan, for the Clean Benza Toilet Fountain: 'What's this, someone's posterior? No, it's a peach, and the toilet fountain is gently washing it in warm water. Is it too much to want something like this yourself?'

From Finland: 'Harry was a very ordinary guy. He wanted a little bit of madness in his life.' (He came to the right place.) From other countries we have the dancing hamburger, and a talking toilet wearing false eyelashes and lipstick.

Then it's over to the French: 'The bowl of soup which is really soup takes some young people on a trip in a flying car over an imaginary town.'

Finally, from those wonderful folks who gave you Pearl Harbor, we bring you: 'The manufacturer of pharmaceuticals teaches us a lot about nature. Animals maintain their health by living in harmony with nature. The elephant's vigorous fart shows just how healthy its diet is.'

However vigorous it was, it would certainly have been healthier than the International Advertising Film Festival in Cannes.

OVERHEARD IN CHAIRMAN'S OFFICE

'The board and I have decided we don't like the colour of your eyes.'

OVERHEARD ON LOCATION

TV PRODUCER TO HIS ASSISTANT, WHO IS DROWNING AFTER HIS BOAT HAS OVERTURNED: 'Throw me the petty cash!'

OVERHEARD AT AGENCY PARTY

'Cocaine is nature's way of saying that you earn too much.'

They Came in Search of Paradise . . .

'Camera open on a long, sun-lit, Caribbean beach,' the script reads, 'palm trees swaying gently against a cloudless sky of brilliant cobalt blue . . .'

It's called a 'trip', ladies and gentlemen – an overseas shoot with lashings of sun, sea, surf and sand, and more beautiful, luscious, mouth-wateringly scrumptious chargeable expenses than you ever dreamed possible.

Every self-respecting creative tries to sell a 'trip' script at least once a year. They don't always succeed. At one client presentation, the creative team proudly started to read out their script. 'Camera opens on beach in Caribbean,' said the copywriter. 'Oh no it doesn't,' said the client. The film was eventually shot at Shepperton.

Convincing a client who makes vacuum cleaners that the benefits of his product will be best dramatised in a commercial involving Robinson Crusoe and Girl Friday on a desert island somewhere in the Bahamas is a real art.

Here is a short checklist of the 'trip' hotels in which you're most likely to rub shoulders with creative directors.

In Venice: The Cipriani or the Gritti Palace.

In the south of France: La Colombe d'Or or the Cap-Eden Roc

In Beverly Hills: The Beverly Wilshire or the Beverly Hills Hotel

In Marbella: Los Monteros or the Puente Romano

In Sydney: The Regent Sydney or Sebel Town House

In the Bahamas: Windermere Island Hotel And Club

In Bermuda: Cambridge Beaches or Lantana Colony Club

In Barbados: Cobblers Cove or Coral Reef Club

In Mombasa: Serene Beach Hotel

In Mexico: Pierre Marques Princess Hotel and Club De Golf, Acapulco

Anywhere else, darling, and it just can't be called a trip.

'Awaydays' are sort of mini-trips. Every have-it-awayday trails a story or two in its wake – everything from the size of the bill for a wrecked hotel lounge to the bill for simply eating and drinking the place hollow.

One enterprising creative team chose Paris for an awayday, to work on a food commercial. They had an exceedingly good time. Bored by their lack of progress by the first afternoon, and urged on by the range and variety of wines and cognacs that they had tested over lunch, they phoned a French model agency and said that they were in Paris to cast models for a shower commercial. The French were impressed by the name of the creative team's agency – and by the fact that they were staying in a £200-a-night suite at the Hotel Ritz. Within an hour, the first models started to arrive, and they continued to arrive until late in the evening. In all, some thirty-seven French beauties came up to the room, removed their blouses and bras, and gave the audience a twirl. Like the professional casters they were, the team recorded each girl's performance with the aid of a Polaroid camera. To this day, those Polaroids are a treasured possession, whilst in Paris there are probably thirty-seven young lovelies with complexes about why their bosoms are so unsuitable for shower commercials.

The awayday that was to produce one of Britain's most famous pieces of advertising was Terry Lovelock's little jaunt to Marrakesh in 1973. Lovelock had been given the job of writing the new Heineken campaign by his boss at Collett Dickenson Pearce, Frank Lowe. The brief was just one word: 'Refreshment'. Around it, Lovelock – and Lovelock alone – was instructed to create a simple, persuasive, and memorable campaign that could run and run: a campaign 'with legs'. That is the CDP way – to take good people, to give them a brief, and then to leave them to get on with it.

Lovelock grappled with the problem for eight weeks without coming remotely close to cracking it – apart from at one stage coming up with the rather amusing idea of a mythical country named after the lager, with the slogan: 'Heineken – What a State to be in'.

In sheer desperation, he decided to refresh his brain by taking a stroll around the block, down the road to Heathrow, and onto a plane to Marrakesh. Quite understandable in the circumstances, you will say, and fairly standard procedure – except that the morning of his departure was also the morning on which Frank Lowe was rather expecting to be having a meeting to review progress. He was less than ecstatic when he read the note that Lovelock had left on his desk: 'Gone to Marrakesh. Back soon.' Seizing the phone, he paged the runaway copywriter in Departures and uttered words to the effect that if he came back to London empty-handed, it might be wiser for his own comfort and safety if he found another planet to live on.

And so it was, at 3am the following morning in his room at the luxurious Hotel Mamounia, that Terry Lovelock woke up suddenly, reached for the pad that writers always keep by their beds, and feverishly scribbled the immortal words: 'Heineken refreshes the parts other beers cannot reach.' The rest, of course, is history.

OVERHEARD IN CANNES

'I must have got back to the hotel all right because I woke up there this morning . . . at least, I think it was me.'

OVERHEARD AT MOSCOW'S

'As an account handler he's so obsequious, we know him as the man who just can't take yes for an answer . . .'

Legal, Decent, Honest and Truthful

FACT NO. 1

Remember the commercial for John Smith's bitter in 1982 that featured a dog doing handstands and a neat line in juggling?

Well the dog was called Becky, and if there was one thing she was totally incapable of doing, it was to perform a handstand by balancing on her front paws. The production company had to come to her rescue by having a pair of false dog's legs specially made for the sequence.

And if there was one other thing that Becky couldn't do, it was juggle. So for that particular sequence, a professional juggler had to hide himself on the other side of the bar and do Becky's juggling for her.

This, in turn, threw up a whole new set of problems. The actor who played 'Arkwright' (the late, very talented, and sadly missed, Gordon Rollins) simply couldn't keep a straight face while Becky's tricks were being performed down by his feet. In fact he was so overcome that the director had to resort to two separate shoots – first of Arkwright and his mate talking, then of the dog's tricks – and then matt the films together.

FACT NO. 2

In the early days of tungsten lighting, food photographers used to get up to all sorts of tricks.

Dumplings would float mouth-wateringly in stews, buoyed up by a raft of implanted corks. Vegetables would float in soup, buoyed up by marbles.

Bubbles would twinkle at the brim of a wine glass – courtesy, invariably, of a tiny glass bead.

Mashed potato would be used instead of ice cream, because it didn't melt under the heat of the studio lights. Shaving foam would be used instead of whipped cream, and what poured so deliciously out of the carton would be not double cream, but white gloss paint.

With new technology, of course – not to mention new legislation – you could be forgiven for thinking that these practices had stopped. Er . . .

In the old days, Whitbread Pale Ale used to photograph better than any other beer in the business. So no matter which brew was being advertised, the canny lensman would always use Whitbread for best results. No modern photographer would sink to such depths, of course. He might use cold tea instead of whisky, and Campari instead of red wine, because the substitutes look better under the camera than the real thing, but – switch beer brands? Never!

What, though, does any up-to-date photographer worth his salt use to rejuvenate fizzy drinks that are sagging under hot studio lights? The answer is, salt. Just a tiny pinch of ordinary table salt is enough to add a refreshing looking stream of bubbles to the unfizziest glass. So does a judicious sprinkling of Vichy crystals. (Here's a little test to prove adman not speak with forked tongue. Next time you're in the pub, simply add a spoonful of salt to your mate's lager. Then stand well back and admire what will closely resemble the lava flows from Vesuvius . . .) If salt or crystals still don't produce the desired effect, the photographer will forcibly aerate the flat liquid by taking the aerator from his goldfish tank, dangling it in the glass, and giving a short, sharp blow.

If the product is champagne or lager, the photographer will also first cloud the glass with wax aerosol to simulate frosting, then mist it over with tiny water droplets from a plant-spray for a photogenically moody, condensation type effect. The finishing touch, a delicious head of bubbles, will come straight from a bottle of washing-up liquid.

When it comes to snapping food, the story is no different. Delicacies such as waffles or pancakes which need syrup as an accompaniment will find themselves swimming instead in a gallon of pure engine oil – because the camera finds it more attractive. And before their final bake, pies, tarts and other pastries will often be glazed with shampoo in order to achieve the 100 per cent yummy glisten effect we consumers demand.

There is, however – you'll be pleased to hear – no need for mashed potato any more. Not when you can use dry ice to keep scoops of ice cream rock hard until you need them. (If, that is, real ice cream is used at all. As in the case of bacon, eggs, toast, orange juice, hamburgers, chips, vegetables, steaks and just about every other food being photographed these days, it is just as likely to be a beautifully moulded and painted wax model from Replica Food Ltd. Or, as in the case of that piece of hot cheese that is stretched between two breaking halves of pizza on our TV screens to spell out the name of the pizza house, for wax read: latex rubber).

Ah, you will say wistfully, but what about all that appetising steam we see – surely that can't be fake? Well, actually, the chances are that it's either a mixture of hydrochloric acid and ammonium chloride, or cigarette smoke blown through a straw. Real steam, believe it or not, evaporates too quickly.

And what about those gorgeous, plump-to-bursting bangers that we see so often on poster hoardings, those last bastions of all that is great in British cuisine? Sorry, hate to tell you, but they've been gently poached in water for half a minute or so to make them nice and swollen, and then they have been lovingly brushed with a succulent coating of teak or mahogany wood dye. And if *that* isn't quite glossy enough, then it's on with the polyurethane.

Bon appetit!

FACT NO. 3

Chop-chop, busy-busy, work-work, bang-bang ... Great commercial, but how on earth, you might ask, did they get that penguin to chat so avidly into the telephone? After the problems of building a complete film set inside a penguin sanctuary in the Cotswolds, sticking a dollop of fish paste onto the handset to make the penguin put his face near it was a comparatively easy task ...

FACT NO. 4

The Greenpeace anti-fur cinema commercial starts glamorously, with fur coated models slinking along the catwalk. Then things get rather horrible when one of the girls drags a fur coat which leaves a trail of blood behind it, and spectators and models alike get drenched in blood. But the experience was not as unpleasant as you might think for the hundred or so volunteers who gave up two days of their time to help make the film. That's because the six gallons of stage blood that splattered all over them was a mixture of food colouring and edible syrup and was, apparently, very very tasty.

FACT NO. 5

The camera never lies, especially when it comes to taking decent photographs for a car ad. That's why it's standard practice to put weights in the boot and bonnet of the car to lower its body onto the wheels. And it's why just about every car ad that is photographed on location is shot either just before dawn or just before dusk – because the low-level light at those times tends to bring out the finer points of the vehicle's metalwork, whilst still producing a 'warm' and 'muted' shot.

But prize for the best car trick must go to top photographer John Claridge, commissioned to shoot a campaign for the Rolls-Royce Silver Spirit, to run in Britain. The setting, however, was Death Valley, and the only car available was a left-hand drive American model. Claridge's elegant solution to the problem was to replace the American twin headlights with British single units, and during the processing stage, to convert left-hand drive to right-hand drive by simply reversing the film.

FACT NO. 6

In one of the commercials for Courage Best bitter, there is a fat old lady who performs an amazing snooker trick, involving potting a ball off several cushions – in front of our very eyes. Now, as the production company discovered, there aren't many fat old ladies around who can even play the game, let alone produce such a stunning shot.

The answer? Fans of 'Pot Black' who watch the commercial closely enough might just make out the style of the great Fred Davis, heavily padded and his face shielded by a large hat.

FACT NO. 7

When a commercial calls for a snake, it is invariably a python that gets the starring role. Not because Equity deems them worthy of lower repeat fees or anything, but because they're so much easier to work with. And as any director will tell you, that's because if you pop a python into the fridge for a few minutes before filming, you couldn't hope for a more cooperative actor . . .

FACT NO. 8

Many products that you might think have traditions as long as your arm were, in fact, invented by clever admen on behalf of their clients. Baileys Irish Cream was concocted in 1975 by a pair or marketing men with a company in Greek Street, Soho, called Innovation and Developement. Briefed by their client to come up with a totally new drink, they eventually hit on the heady mixture of cream, chocolate and spirits that we know and love. Their formula was soon turned into a marketable brew by one of the client company's scientists, and in the search for a product name the inventive duo had to look no further than the restaurant directly beneath their offices; an elegant eaterie called – you guessed it – Baileys.

FACT NO. 9

Who said Things Go Better With Coke? In developing countries, it seems, douching with The Real Thing is a widely acccepted form of birth control. The Harvard Medical School researched the admirably creative practice, and reported its findings in a letter to the *New England Journal of Medicine* in November 1985. Entitled 'Effect of "Coke" on Sperm Mobility', the report detailed how the scientists had added sperm specimens to different formulations of Coca Cola, to see how many of the little chaps would stop wriggling after one minute. Classic Coke was impressive, stopping all movement in 91 percent of cases. Diet Coke was positively lethal, stopping every little sperm stone dead. 'Coca Cola products do appear to have a spermicidal effect,' the Harvard boffins concluded. 'Furthermore, our data indicate that at least in the area of spermicidal effect, "classic" coke is it.'

'We do not promote Coca-Cola for medical purposes,' said a highly humorous company spokesman. 'It is a soft drink.'

No wonder the slogan 'Coke Adds Life' fell from favour.

OVERHEARD IN COPTIC STREET

'The merger of Masius with Benton and Bowles? It's like airlifting passengers off the Titanic in the Hindenburg.'

OVERHEARD AT THE LAMB AND FLAG

'As a friend, I'll level with you. The other printer always gets our business because he showed a better understanding of our problems by leaving a new Merc outside my house and shoving the registration documents through the letter box.'

Hiccups, Cock-ups and Did Anyone Remember to Take Out Insurance?

No. 1

In 1983, the Guardian reported the results of a £10,000 anti-vandal campaign on South Yorkshire buses.

It seems that so good was the advertising – by an unnamed (and I'm not surprised) agency – that it produced an increase in damage to the buses in question of no less than 20 per cent.

No. 2

You don't have to be a BMW owner to remember that impressive commercial where a gleaming 7 Series weaves its way through a misty, sinister graveyard of dead American cars, each upright in the ground as if part of a latter-day Stonehenge.

Beautifully shot, on location, at great expense.

Pity the end-frames capture for ever the antics of a bumble bee that's flying across the lens.

No. 3

The advertising poster for Zube cough sweets that was being sent to Saudi Arabia looked innocent enough. A large picture of a horse, with the award-winning headline: 'Are you Hoarse? Go Suck A Zube.' But the translator anticipated problems with the Saudi authorites. Why was that, asked the agency? Because, replied the translator, Zube may be a cough sweet in English, but in Arabic it's slang for 'penis'.

And just a few years ago, the Commercial Union proudly opened a new office in Rio and had the giant letters CU installed on the top of the building for all to see. Two days later they had the giant letters CU hurriedly taken down for all not to see. For, as a prospective client had been kind enough to point out to them, in local dialect their company initials spell out the gutter slang for the female pudendum . . .

No. 4

In one of their Guinnless commercials for Guinness, Allen Brady and Marsh depicted the town of Weymouth and managed to call it Skegness. This so outraged the hoteliers and publicans of the Dorset seaside resort that they banned the sale of Guinness for a month. The wound was healed only when Guinness handed over a nice cheque as a goodwill gesture.

No. 5

A few years ago, the last item on 'News At Ten' showed horrifying footage of a crashed airliner. The programme ended, the credits rolled, and on came a commercial. For the very airline whose plane had been involved . . .

No. 6

An issue of *Living* magazine carried a tasty looking double page advertisement for Sharwood's curry. 'Making a curry is simple,' the headline stated, 'compared with making the curry powder.' All fine and good, especially when accompanied by a one-page recipe for a delicious Indian dish. Except that when readers turned the page, they were greeted with an editorial feature that read: 'NOW FOR SOME *REAL* CURRY.'

No. 7

Awards for The Most Unbelievable Cock-Up By Whoever It Is That Puts Up Posters
Imagine two large poster sites, side by side.
One, booked by Homefire, with a poster that reads: 'Homefire, Unbelievably hot.'
The other, booked by the GLC Public Safety campaign, with a poster that reads; 'Stop the home fires burning.'

First prize must go to this one:

Two large poster sites again, side by side.

One carried a public service message about sexually transmitted diseases, with the headline: 'VD – The Deadly Disease.'

The other one simply read: 'I Got It At The Co-Op.'

No. 8

An agency that shall remain nameless made what was surely *the* prize cock-up in 1983, when they ran an ad in a charity brochure for the deaf with the headline: 'Now hear this . . .'

No. 9

Bet you were wondering when we were going to tell you the famous Strand story. Well, here it is.

In 1960, the agency S.H. Benson were asked by their client W.D. & H.O. Wills to come up with a campaign for a new, cheap filter cigarette called Strand.

Benson's decided to appeal to the younger market by associating the cigarette with the loneliness and rejection of youth. A 28-year-old actor called Terence Brook, who looked like a cross between Frank Sinatra and James Dean, was cast for the starring role in the campaign.

The commercial showed him in a late night London fog, strolling gloomily past large stone buildings in deserted streets. Raincoat collar turned up until it nearly met the rim of his Homburg, Brook stepped into the light shed by a solitary street lamp, smiled wryly, and lit up a Strand. Inhaling deeply, he then strolled back into the darkness of the night.

The campaign was a smash hit. Before you could even say 'cock-up', Terence Brook had his own fan club. Music from the commercial – 'The Lonely Man Theme' – hit the charts, a slow, haunting big-band arrangement that featured a plaintive harmonica as lead instrument.

The client had just one little niggle with the agency: nobody was buying any of the product. 'You're never alone with a Strand,' said the male voice-over; in the public's mind, as research later proved, this had become: 'Loneliness is a cigarette called Strand'. They stayed away in droves.

A few years ago, the person in charge of an office equipment supplier's promotions had a bright idea for selling more shredding machines. He prepared a mail-shot, addressed it to board directors of major companies, posted it on Thursday, and went away for a well-deserved long weekend.

The mailer consisted of a single sheet of cheap lined writing paper, on which one Mavis Blogg, cleaner, had written a threatening letter. Our Mrs Blogg was in possession of certain company secrets, discovered in the recipient's waste-paper basket, and if she did not receive the sum of £500 by Monday, she'd tell all to the company's competitors.

Now the promotions executive intended to follow up this first letter the very next day with the mail-shot proper, stating that it would be clear from the Mavis Blogg scare that company secrets should be shredded before they fell into the wrong hands. Indeed, his secretary sent them out exactly on schedule.

But by Friday afternoon, all hell had been let loose. It appeared that by a cruel quirk of fate, Mavis Blogg was the real name of the cleaner who worked for one of the mail-shot recipients. Assuming the threats to be real, he took the appropriate action, and poor Mavis Blogg was hauled off in a Black Maria. Luckily the police believed her story, and Mavis was released.

But Mrs Blogg was by now making some dark threats of her own, against persons unknown. And as soon as the second mail-shot arrived on Saturday morning, with the shredding company's address, she went on the war-path.

To cut a long story into very short and embarrassing shreds, the promotions executive found his long weekend – though luckily not his career – very much curtailed. Mrs Blogg was steered away from litigation only with the aid of a cheque for, appropriately, the sum of £500.

OVERHEARD DOWNSTAIRS AT LANGAN'S

'A freelance creative consultant is someone brought in at the last minute to share the blame.'

No. 11

The New York magazine *Magazine Age* sent out an effusive sales letter to prospective advertisers in 1984. The letter didn't work too well in Britain, though, perhaps because of the writer's less than profound knowledge of English idioms: extolling the drive and enthusiasm of the journal's staff, he rather unnervingly stated that they worked so hard that, 'As our editor says, "every month we try to top ourselves".'

No. 12

The chocolate bar was called Aztec, so of course the creative team had written a commercial set amongst ruins in South Mexico. A brown and muscular Aztec warrior climbs slowly up the face of a giant pyramid, at the top of which sit the gods in all their glory. The pyramid's steps jut out just a few inches, yet the warrior has to remain upright as he climbs. At the top he offers up a large wooden bowl to the gods, and at that point a spectacular flight of white doves is released in the brilliant sunlight. It was a very tricky piece of action to film, but the final effect was stunning. When the agency tested the public's reaction to the finished commercial, a 'man in the street' described it thus: 'Well, there's this coloured geezer climbing up the side of a building, and when he gets to the top they chuck snowballs at him.'

OVERHEARD AT MOSCOW'S

'Doing business with that agency is like wearing a condom. One gets a feeling of pleasure and security, whilst being screwed.'

OVERHEARD IN RECEPTION

'The Orient Express leaves for Venice at noon. Be under it.'

No. 13

Many years back, Unilever tried to launch a washing powder called Omo in Kenya. (You know, the one that bored house-wives used to leave in their windows at army bases in Germany, because its initials stood for Old Man Out . . .) Anyway, the product bombed. Unilever were puzzled, and so was its agency – especially as research had shown almost total acceptance of give-away trial packs.

More research was commissioned, and a rather interesting fact came to light. Almost every potential female consumer of the product in Kenya was in the habit of doing her washing down by the riverside. Many had tried Omo, and without fail, they all reported the powder's annoying habit of floating away with the current before they had time to start scrubbing . . . the traditional bar of soap won every time.

With typical pizzazz, however, the agency cracked the problem by giving away a free bowl with every pack, together with detailed instructions.

No. 14

A famous pet-food manufacturer once tried bringing out a rehydratable dog food that combined the convenience of a dried format with the tasty goodness of the usual tinned variety. The product performed stunningly well in concept research, but rather fell down when marketed for real, for three reasons:

1. It wasn't convenient. You 'just added boiling water', but then had to wait several minutes while it cooled down. Meanwhile, the smell was driving the dog crazy with desire.

2. When the big moment arrived, the dog went even crazier. Dogs don't like hot food.

3. Nor do they like diarrhoea, which is what the product gave them.

FROM THE MOST HONEST INTERNAL MEMO OF ALL TIME

'Client rejected copy he had written at previous meeting.'

A commercial made for Cinzano in 1984 cost the client rather more than the original budget had allowed for. So what's new, you might ask? But at least this time the excuse was rather more exotic than usual, and three of the clients were actually present to verify it. Shot on location in Italy, the commercial's end frames are of a massive party where everybody is enjoying their glass of Cinzano. To make sure they got the 1,000 or so 'guests' that would be required to make the shot authentic, the director and crew put posters up all over the location village, just north of Venice, inviting the inhabitants to come and enjoy a few free glasses of aperitif. It was a big party all right. Word of mouth advertising had worked so well that no fewer than 6,000 would-be revellers arrived on the set. To the client's eternal credit, every single one of them was allowed to join in the festivities.

No. 16

When Ogilvy and Mather were looking for a smart, up-market location for a British Gas still shoot, someone suggested the Thames-side apartment belonging to Jeffrey Archer. Be my guest, said Archer: the fee for two hours' use will be a mere few thousand pounds, to be sent to a charity of my choice.

Bye, said the agency, and off they set to find another location. Their travels took them as far as the next flight of stairs, to an empty apartment on the floor above.

History does not relate which peeved Mr Archer more – the loss of a few thousand pounds for his charity, or the noisy arrival of several fire engines and firemen when the hot photographic lamps set off the building's fire sprinklers . . .

OVERHEARD IN AGENCY IN-HOUSE WINE BAR

'Me and De Bono – we think alike.'

No. 17

Advertising posters seem to bring out the best in British graffiti. The Whitehall Theatre of War in London once displayed a large photograph of Winston Churchill on one of its outside walls. Some brilliant wag wrote underneath it: 'We aren't allowed to advertise war, so here's a Winston.'

A poster in Ireland read: '7 Million Guinnesses Are Drunk Every Day'. Within hours, some wit had added, 'I never knew there were so many piss-artists in the family.'

A poster for the Fiat 127 proudly told us that 'If it were a woman, it would get its bottom pinched'. Some feminist took umbrage of course, and added; 'If this woman was a car, she would run you down.' The poster, complete with graffito, is now a best-selling postcard.

No. 18

It could only happen in America. The Elliot-Hamil Funeral Home in Abilene, Texas, sued the Southwestern Bell Telephone Company for $3000,000 after the phone company had mixed up its yellow pages entries a little and listed the funeral home under 'Frozen Foods – Wholesale.'

OVERHEARD IN PRESENTATION ROOM

AGENCY CHAIRMAN TO PROSPECTIVE CLIENT, AFTER THREE HOURS OF CREATIVE PRESENTATION: 'And now perhaps I can offer you a glass of something?'

YAWNING PROSPECTIVE CLIENT: 'That's the best idea I've heard all morning.'

OVERHEARD IN AGENCY BOARDROOM

JOURNALIST TO AGENCY FOUNDER: 'Who would you most like to be, if not yourself?'

ACENCY FOUNDER: 'My wife.'

OVERHEARD IN PARK LANE

AGENCY FOUNDER TO CABBIE, WHOSE TAXI THE AGENCY LIMO HAS JUST CUT UP: 'Go away, or I'll have you killed.'

OVERHEARD IN COVENT GARDEN

GUEST AFTER DINNER IN HOST'S CHOICE OF RESTAURANT: 'I don't think it's worth having coffee here, do you?'

The Sign-Off

And finally, here is a selection of stories, anecdotes and first-hand accounts that have taken their rightful place in advertising myth and legend.

★When the production team for the famous Benson & Hedges 'Swimming Pool' cinema commercial arrived in Los Angeles, they telephoned ahead to the location in Phoenix to make sure that someone had ordered the forty iguanas that were required on the shoot.

But someone, somewhere, got their wires seriously crossed, and when the director, Hugh Hudson, walked on to the set on the first day of filming, he was nearly knocked off his feet by forty excited, yapping and highly boisterous chihuahuas . . .

Never mind, there was plenty of time in which to rectify the mistake. The team spent the next four days sitting in the rain, watching the entire area being slowly flooded – for the first time in about two hundred years.

★A few of the boys fell foul of the cocoa leaf on one shoot in darkest Peru. They'd gone to the foothills of the Andes to get the perfect shot of a llama with a road disappearing off into the horizon, for a poster that was to appear on motorway bridges all over Britain. (Yes, you're right: at 70 mph a stock shot of a llama superimposed on a stock shot of a mountain road would have done the trick. But anyway . . .)

Now the thing about llamas is that they don't live in the foothills of the Andes; they live rather near the summits.

Undeterred, and mindful of the large sums of money already spent to get even this far, the photographer and agency team hired a few local sherpas to take them up into llama country. As they climbed, the locals chewed steadily on cocoa leaves. And when they offered some to the gringos, it seemed bad manners not to accept. By the time they got high enough to see a llama, the photographer was practically in orbit.

To cut a long but beautiful story short, reliable sources have put the cost of the shoot at just a little under a quarter of a million pounds. For this, the client received one 3 inch × 3 inch transparency, which then had to be superimposed on a separate shot of a mountain road. The client's reaction was not recorded.

★When British Rail put its account up for grabs a few years back, the client team (including Sir Peter Parker and other luminaries) arrived at one agency's reception at the appointed time to find it awash with dirty coffee cups and filthy ash-trays. Sir Peter was told by the receptionist to sit down and wait: the agency team would be along in a minute. The minute became five minutes, and five minutes became a quarter of an hour.

When the BR chairman at last went back to the reception desk, he was sullenly told that someone was ill, and that someone else had failed to turn up. No one was offered refreshments, or made to feel welcome in any way. Finally, after thirty minutes, an irate BR team headed for the door . . . at the exact moment that the agency team made its entrance – and said that perhaps the British Rail bosses now knew what it felt like to be a British Rail passenger. The agency got the business on the spot.

Great, aren't they? Adpeople and groupies recount them with zest at the Zanzibar, with gusto at the Gavroche. And they should have happened that way. But each is entirely mythical and legendary. Not legal, decent, honest or truthful at all. That's advertising.

OVERHEARD AT A CASTING SESSION

TV PRODUCER TO REJECTED ACTRESS: 'I'm sorry, but
you look too old.'

AND AFTER CALLING HER BACK, HAVING BEEN TOLD
HIS COMMENT WAS RATHER HARSH: 'Sorry, what I
really meant to say was that you're not attractive enough.'

Glossary

A To see how easily advertising manipulates you, simply turn to 'Z'.

AB/C1/C2/DE The four most commonly used definitions of socio-economic class, *qv* Punter.

Adaptation Someone else's ad, modified to fit your brief.

Allen, Joe Good place to impress a spinach and bacon salad.

Analysis, Cluster (i) Research technique used by planners in agencies to test your product's viability.

(ii) Research technique used by secretaries in the backs of cabs, to test your product's viability, *qv* Research, Dipstick.

Breakdown, Readership Analysis of readership statistics.

Breakdown, Cost Analysis of agency bill (*qv* Figure, Ball-park).

Breakdown, Nervous Analysis of creative director.

Brief, Creative (i) Document issued to members of creative department, granting the bearer unhindered passage to Barbados or LA.

(ii) Consultant in wig retained to liaise with Inland Revenue.

Cannes Venue for annual advertising works outing. Also, French for '£140 a bottle'.

Cash Means of getting film crew to finish shoot before going into overtime, *qv* Plastic (money).

Chairman *qv* ZZZs.

Commission Warrant granted to member of Her Majesty's armed forces before he goes into account handling at JWT.

Curling The art of picking up a restaurant bill, paying the date by mistake, and not batting an eyelid.

D&AD Designers' & Art Directors' Association. Awarders of golds and silvers, love.

E, The big *qv* 'Envelopes, Night of the long'.

Expenses, Doing Your What accounts for 40 per cent of Hours, Chargeable.

Figure, Ball park Estimate of agency bill, divided by two.

Filofax Portable personal organiser. (Does *yours* have the international temperature directory?)

Freelance Means of boosting one's salary from the merely stratospheric to the simply extra-terrestial.

Grand, Forty Minimum living wage.

Klein, Calvin Purveyor of underpants to 99 per cent of adwomen.

LA Eleven hours from LHR.

Langan's Mayfair snack bar.

L'Escargot Good place to impress a bottle of Perrier (*qv*).

Marlboro Packet seen in breast pocket of art director's short-sleeved Hawaiian shirt.

MEAL Advertising expenditure, monitored by Media Expenditure Analysis Ltd.

Meal Power breakfast, working lunch, strategic dinner – advertising consumption of, unmonitored.

Oxfam Couturier by appointment to copywriters everywhere.

Penetration Refreshing the parts. Often the result of effective Research, Dipstick (*qv*).

Perrier What to drink in L'Escargeau.

Plastic (money) Not accepted by film crews. *qv* Cash.

Plastic (people) Have a nice day.

Porsche A brand of sunglasses and multi-function chronometers.

Punter You.

Recall, Aided Research technique whereby subjects are told exactly which aspects of your ad they are likely to hate the most.

Research, Dipstick Useful technique for gauging a subject's reaction to a creative proposal, before shelling out £50 on her at the Neal Street Restaurant, *qv* Analysis, Cluster.

Retoucher Important member of art department, whose airbrush can magically extend the life of your season ticket by at least another month.

Seymour 0.8 of a White (*qv*).

Shoot, Photographic – as in 'I'll be on a shoot all day tomorrow': Day off.

Type A Thrusting adperson, *qv* Penetration.

USM Place in City where agency founders go to become millionaires.

Vice-president One of 456 people at Ogilvy & Mather.

White 1.2 Seymours (*qv*).

Zanzibar Cocktail bar where secretaries go to say 'absolutely' a lot.

Zippo Smelly item found next to Marlboro packet (*qv*).

ZZZs Catch some, don't mind if I do: *qv* Chairman.

Ziessen To accept an invitation to lunch to discuss a book about advertising and then to insist on picking up the bill oneself, *qv* L'Escargot, *qv* Langan's, *qv* LA.

Z To see how easily advertising manipulates you, simply turn to 'A'.